The Diary of a Shirtwaist Striker

Theresa Serber Malkiel

Introductory essay by Françoise Basch

ILR Press
an imprint of
Cornell University Press
Ithaca and London

Contents

Foreword

When I first read Theresa Serber Malkiel's *Diary of a Shirtwaist Striker* in the late 1970s, I found her story spellbinding. Through her fictional narrative, she had brought to life her own experience as an eyewitness to the 1909 "Uprising of the 20,000" on New York's Lower East Side. A Jewish immigrant from Russia, a labor activist, a socialist militant, and an experienced journalist, Theresa Malkiel was well equipped to provide this firsthand account of the strike.

Almost no one can remain indifferent to the theme of the story. The strikers, or "girls" as they were called, brought the shirtwaist industry to a halt for thirteen weeks in 1909–10, resisting a united front of employers, judges, lawyers, and police. The young women, most of them recent immigrants from Eastern Europe and Italy, were unskilled, untutored in English, and unorganized.

Surprisingly, in the late 1970s, no historian had treated this heroic episode in depth. Although the strike was mentioned here and there, the main issues were ignored. Historians discussed the strike in relation to other events, such as the fire that devastated the Triangle Waist Company in March 1911 or as the prelude to the vaster, "better organized" cloakmakers' strike of 1911. Stereotypes prevailed in the condescending representations of the women strikers as helpless victims or as brave but unorganized workers. For the most part, these historians ignored gender as well as ethnic specificity.[1]

My presentation of Malkiel's *Diary* in 1980 to French readers belonged to the first wave, as it were, of feminist history, or "her-story." I had three primary aims: to rescue invisible women from the shadows, to highlight their historical agency and heroism, and to articulate their complex identities as workers, women, and immigrants within the context of contemporary social and political forces.[2]

Now, ten years later, feminist historians have produced a rich and sophisticated historiography of the shirtwaist makers' strike that reflects the new theoretical concerns of women's history. While gender is a key parameter of their approach, they also place events in a broader social and political context. In the case of the shirtwaist makers' strike, this means linking in a cohesive pattern the several dimensions of women's lives, including the workplace, the home and family, and their ethnic groups. Indeed, recent studies focus on the interaction of gender, ethnicity, and class not only as important but as critical to understanding the strikers' complex strategies and their problematic alliances with labor unions, socialists, and middle-class feminists.

This new comprehensive approach examines work, society, and home as linked spheres, not as autonomous areas. One study, for instance, stresses the influence of women's community networks and daily lives on female militancy, encompassed in the symbol of "bread and roses." Oral histories of immigrant women highlight the importance of cultural heritage in working-class

---

1. Joan M. Jensen and Ann Schofield have documented this bias among early labor historians and their lack of interest in the needle trades. See Jensen and Davidson, *A Needle, a Bobbin, a Strike*, 86, 173.

2. See Joan Wallach Scott's discussion in Scott and Hufton, "Women in History," 145–46. The third aim concerns such recent goals as the "rewriting of history."

history.[3] Still other studies focus on class and ethnicity as they relate to the problem of "Americanization" and on the ways in which immigrants absorbed and resisted American life.[4]

Concern with class and gender inspires questions about the impact of female industrial activism on labor unions, including, for example, the long-term effects of the shirtwaist makers' strike and the change in the International Ladies' Garment Workers' Union from a craft to an industrial union.[5]

Accounts of the socialist women's movement and of the National Women's Trade Union League place the strike in the context of the history of labor, of women's and radical movements at the turn of the century, and of middle-class reformism. The emphasis in these social histories is on the connection between industrial and political action and women's suffrage.[6]

In short, women's history has come a long way, and the shirtwaist makers' strike is a significant illustration of many trends in that history.

For many years, scholars dismissed *The Diary of a Shirtwaist Striker* as mere propaganda. Yet, as emotional and naive as Malkiel's fable sometimes strikes us, it highlights the political and symbolic meaning of the drama and the characters. In the essay that follows, I discuss the strike in the context of class, ethnicity, and gender and analyze how Theresa Malkiel creates journalistic fiction that promotes socialism. I begin with a discussion of the strikers' work and home lives. I then examine the supporters of the strike and the sequence of events. From here, I move to a discussion of Theresa Serber Malkiel as militant and author and, finally, to an analysis of the fictional account of the strike as presented in *The Diary of a Shirtwaist Striker.*

---

3. Ewen, *Immigrant Women in the Land of Dollars;* Cameron, "Bread and Roses Revisited."

4. See, among others, Kessler-Harris, "Organizing the Unorganizable."

5. Waldinger, "Another Look at the ILGWU."

6. Buhle, *Women and American Socialism;* Dye, *As Sisters and as Equals.*

I wish to thank several people who helped me in my research—Alice Kessler-Harris, Elinor Lerner, Lillian Robinson, Dorothy Swanson, and Barbara Wertheimer—and Sonia Farber and Pauline Newman, who worked in the shirtwaist trade and agreed to be interviewed. Many thanks also to those who kindly read parts or all of the manuscript—Leora Auslander, Joan Dupont, Barbara Karsky, and Claudia Koonz—and to Catherine Cullen, who translated the original French text into English before I did my adaptation.

Françoise Basch

The Shirtwaist Strike in History and Myth

Françoise Basch

The Shirtwaist Girls at Home and at Work

*T*he Diary of a Shirtwaist Striker created a legend about "girls" who became both heroines and pioneers of socialist ideals. But more than just hagiography, the book recounted a genuine women's rebellion that was a milestone in early twentieth-century labor history. The social and political framework in which the events unfolded was marked by the emergence of industrialization, a substantial increase in the use of female labor, changes in labor organization, massive immigration, and the growth of socialism and feminism.

The strike began on November 22, 1909, at an enthusiastic gathering at Cooper Union in New York City. Within twelve hours fifteen thousand shirtwaist makers had walked out, and a few hours later twenty-five thousand. They did not return to work until February 15, 1910. [1]

The revolt in New York was part of a nationwide industrial protest movement that occurred between 1900 and 1920 and involved one hundred thousand women, most of them immigrants. They walked out in clothing factories in New York City, Chicago, Rochester, Cleveland, and other cities, made similar demands, challenged factory owners, confronted the police, and

---

1. Estimates of the number of strikers vary from twenty thousand to thirty thousand.

turned for support to middle-class women. Joan Jensen has described the period as "an incredible decade, with thousands of working women in the streets demanding economic justice." Besides closed shops, better working conditions, and higher salaries, the women asked for bread and roses and overwhelmed the sedate and sexist male unions: "For two decades, women workers in America—like the women in revolutionary Russia—were a catalyst for worker discontent."[2]

Who were the fearless, spunky "girls" who walked out on the Lower East Side? What inspired them to jeopardize their daily bread to rebel against employers—often friends and relatives—and trust their own resources against powerful adversaries? The workplace—the horrible working conditions and the growth of labor organization—provides only clues to the roots of this massive action, for the women revolted not only as workers but as women and immigrants, in a space that included home, family, and a new city and country. Labor historians have called this space "the bedrock of laboring women's daily lives" where gender and ethnicity intersect with class.[3]

Immigrant Life Many of the Jews who immigrated en masse from Eastern Europe to New York in the 1880s and 1890s sought jobs in the rapidly expanding needle trades, where their skills as tailors, cloak makers, and seamstresses found a natural outlet.[4] The concentration of German-Jewish immigrants in the needle trades and the proliferation of sweatshops facilitated this "great migration." After the economic hardships and pogroms they had suffered in the old country, many of the immigrants were happy to find employment in Jewish establishments where relatives or compatriots had risen to the position of foremen or

---

2. Jensen, "The Great Uprisings," 83.
3. Cameron, "Bread and Roses Revisited," 56.
4. "Of the wage workers, two thirds were employed in the needle trades." Menes, "The East Side and the Jewish Labor Movement," 205–6.

small employers. Sharing a culture and a religion with one's co-workers eased the trauma of uprooting, and the freedom to observe dietary rules and the Jewish holidays was invaluable. Familiar landmarks and human support cushioned the immigrants' head-on confrontation with a foreign and hostile culture.

It soon became clear, however, that many Jewish contractors and bosses took advantage of the helpless immigrants, who were inexperienced in industrial organization and paralyzed by their ignorance of the new country. The comments of one employer were typical: "I want no experienced girl . . . but these greenhorns . . . cannot speak English . . . and they just come from the old country, and I let them work hard, like the devil, for less wages."[5]

Patterns of immigration differed from one ethnic group to another. Anti-Semitic persecution prevented Jewish men from returning to Europe, so they tended to come indefinitely with wives and children and to be considered stable immigrants. From 1886 to 1898, women accounted for 43 percent of the Jewish immigrants. Many of these women knew dressmaking and were soon employed in the needle trades. In contrast, Italian men, "birds of passage," often arrived alone and stayed only temporarily. Women represented only 22 percent of the Italian immigrants.[6]

Landing in New York, the immigrants swarmed to the Lower East Side, "the immigrant Jewish cosmopolis," which, between 1900 and 1905, was the most densely populated area in the United States.[7] Southern Italians and Eastern European Jews merged into "a seething human sea, fed by streams, streamlets and rills of immigration flowing from all the Yiddish-speaking centers of Europe." They joined Germans, Rumanians, and Levantines already living there. From the 1890s on, the Russians

---

5. Quoted in Seidman, *The Needle Trades,* 34.
6. Kessner, *Golden Door,* 32.
7. Ewen, *Immigrant Women,* 26.

arrived in largest numbers, peaking at 259,000 in 1907, and settled between Grand and Monroe streets, "the most densely packed quarter in the city."[8] No wonder Rudyard Kipling compared the Lower East Side to "a Zulu Kraal" and other observers likened it to "the worst sections of Bombay."[9] By 1914, one-sixth of the city's population lived below Fourteenth Street squeezed between offices, factories, and workshops.

The wild urban jungle of the Lower East Side daunted both observers and residents:

> The vista of the New York street is flanked by high rows of brick tenements, fringed with jutting white iron fire escapes, and hung with bulging feather-beds and pillows puffing from the windows. . . . In summertime the children sleep on the steps and on covered chicken coops along the sidewalk; for inside, the rooms are too often small and stifling, some on the inner courts hung with washing, some of them practically closets, without any opening whatever to the outer air.[10]

Tenements went up everywhere. Between seven and nine stories high with at best a toilet and a washbasin per floor or in the yard, the buildings had dark, airless rooms that opened into a foul-smelling yard or air shaft. The inhabitants risked not only asphyxiation but injury or death from fires, for their flimsy fire escapes were often clogged with broken furniture and other refuse and on hot summer nights with bodies.

In the heydays of sweatshops, from 1880 to 1920, tenements were also frequently used for work. In small, overcrowded rooms, "the sewing went forward amid the daily tasks of cooking, cleaning and child rearing."[11]

---

8. Rischin, *Promised City,* 76, 80.
9. Kessner, *Golden Door,* 20.
10. Clark and Wyatt, "Working-Girls' Budgets," 71.
11. Jensen, "The Great Uprisings," 85. Some of Jacob Riis's photographs depict the desperate living conditions in the tenements.

Frequent arrivals, kinship ties, and poverty drove many families to sublet part of their tiny lodgings. "Only millionaires can be alone in America," says one of the characters in Anzia Yezierska's novel *Bread Givers.* [12] The "boarder," a stock figure of Jewish folklore and of the "Bintel Brief," a column in the newspaper the *Jewish Daily Forward,* lived on next to nothing, barely eking out an existence. Irving Howe recounts how the enforced proximity of the tenements caused discomfort as well as domestic dramas. [13]

To shirtwaist maker and future union organizer Pauline Newman, going "home" after work approximated the nightmare of the workshop:

> You got out of the workshop, dark and cold in winter, hot in summer, dirty unswept floors, no ventilation, and you would go home. What kind of home did you go to? . . . I lived in a two-room tenement with my mother and two sisters and the bedroom had no windows, the facilities were down in the yard, but that's the way it was in the factories too. In the summer the sidewalk, fire escapes, and the roof of the tenements became bedrooms just to get a breath of air. We wore cheap clothes, lived in cheap tenements, ate cheap food. There was nothing to look forward to. [14]

In spite of the extreme harshness of life, the Lower East Side was not all bleakness and deprivation. Uprooted and poor, struggling for a place in the sun, the immigrants built a new identity for themselves with extraordinary endurance and vitality, combining a sense of tradition with a determination to assimilate. Morris Hillquit, a socialist lawyer, gave voice to the general excitement and the sense of adventure: "Peals of gay laughter and voices of earnest and animated conversation . . .

---

12. Yezierska, *Bread Givers,* 13.
13. Howe, *World of Our Fathers,* 178.
14. Quoted in Wertheimer, *We Were There,* 295.

from different groups on the roofs. . . . It was a slice of old Russian life that was thus transported to Cherry Street."[15]

The culture and excitement of the Lower East Side also impressed visitors. A Jewish resident of Boston who visited around 1905 noted that his favorite places were the patisseries and cafés, "universities of the ghetto," centers of artistic, intellectual, and political Yiddish life.[16]

In her autobiography, Elizabeth Gurley Flynn, a militant in the radical Industrial Workers of the World, contrasted the dreary South Bronx and the stimulating Jewish district, with its blend of religious traditions and socialism:

> The East Side opened up another world to me, beside which the South Bronx Irish railroad workers and German piano workers drinking their beer in corner saloons seemed sedate and dull. On the East Side, crowded meetings abounded, with animated discussion. . . . The halls were long and narrow, poorly heated and lighted. . . . Usually there was a canopy for Jewish weddings with faded velvet hangings and dusty flowers. On the walls were charters of "landsmen" clubs and beautiful red banners of socialist locals and unions hung carefully under glass and taken out only for special occasions like May Day.[17]

From the 1880s on, taking advantage of a process of secularization and of the virtual disappearance of the most orthodox forms of Judaism, intellectuals preached brotherhood and Marxism, expressed in biblical, even talmudic, rhetoric: "On Pentecost eve 1886, Abraham Cahan compared the socialist message to the giving of the Law on Mount Sinai. . . . Israel's liberation from the Egyptian yoke symbolized the liberation of humanity

---

15. Hillquit, *Loose Leaves*, 2.

16. Howe, *World of Our Fathers*, 235–37. Howe writes eloquently of the richness, diversity, and intensity of Yiddish culture.

17. Flynn, *Rebel Girl*, 67. Landsmen clubs were associations whose members had been inhabitants of the same town or *shtetl*.

as predicted by Isaiah. Hence Jews were urged to join with 'oppressed mankind' in 'the sacred struggle.' "[18]

The failure of the 1905 revolution in Russia and the arrival in 1906 of Bundist militants stimulated the revolutionary ideals of Jewish socialists. Experienced in both union organization and the international workers' movement, the Bundists brought socialist Jews in America a model of secular Yiddish life. [19] Judaism and socialism blended together: "Humanitarianism, brotherhood and progress with its socialist and Judaic glow flowed on in Yiddish New York. To the holidays of the Jewish Calendar were added Labor Day and May Day, the Fourth of July."[20]

Jewish Labor   Against this lively cultural and political setting, the organization of Jewish workers was not as swift as could be expected and discouraged some leaders. Morris Hillquit commented: "The Jewish workers seemed unorganizable. They had not been trained in any form of collective action in the country of their birth. They were dull, apathetic and unintelligent."[21] In his exasperation, Hillquit seemed to ignore the crushing difficulties immigrants encountered in making the transition from the Old to the New World. He was, however, well aware of the sources of the workers' passivity.

The first problem was the immigrants' poverty and ignorance: "Peddlers, workers in the clothing industry, bakers, cigar makers, etc. . . . Their condition of life and labor were pitiful. Ignorant of the language and ways of the country of their adoption . . . they were left at the mercy of their employers, mostly

---

18. Rischin, *Promised City,* 157–58.

19. Ertel, *Le roman juif américain,* 47. The Bund was a Jewish workers' movement that started in Eastern Europe at the end of the nineteenth century. To the left of international socialism, it promoted the Yiddish language and collaboration with national labor movements.

20. Rischin, *Promised City,* 167.

21. Hillquit, *Loose Leaves,* 17.

men of their own race."[22] Immigrants were clearly ready victims for exploitation.

Second, driven by the need to bring their families over from the old country, Jewish immigrants took any job and worked interminable hours. Employers ready to assist a compatriot, finance his passage, offer him a job, or treat him as a relative or dependent provided support, albeit paternalistic and individualistic.

Third, the structure of the clothing industry, which allowed a determined worker to rise to the status of foreman, subcontractor, or boss, rewarded individual rather than collective achievement.

Fourth, and finally, the support networks created for new immigrants, such as landsmen clubs, like family ties and easy promotion, discouraged union organization. So did the ethnic and economic rivalries between immigrants who had arrived at different times and from different countries.[23]

Despite these difficulties, a Jewish labor movement developed alongside the American Federation of Labor (AFL). In 1886, a handful of Jewish intellectuals (Morris Hillquit, Bernard Weinstein, Max Pine, and Abraham Cahan) had founded "the Vereinigte Yiddish Gewerkshaften" (United Hebrew Trades, or UHT). The organization aimed to promote cooperation among Jewish unions in New York, to create new ones, and to spread socialism among Jewish workers.[24] By 1909, just before the Uprising of the 20,000, the UHT had grown from three unions with eighty members to forty-one organizations with five thousand members.[25]

---

22. Ibid., 16
23. For a discussion of the difficulties in organizing Jewish workers, see Rischin, *Promised City*, chap. 9.
24. According to Howe, "Jewish union" usually referred to the needle trades.
25. *Jewish People*, 4:350.

The International Ladies' Garment Workers' Union (ILGWU), founded in 1900 by Joseph Barondess and other workers in the industry, also had difficulties in the beginning. Initially and for some time, it suffered from a scarcity of members and financial penury. A semi-industrial union, the ILGWU was open to all garment workers, whatever their nationality, race, or qualifications. The union was organized into locals by trade and qualifications. Thus a majority of the women workers were in the shirtwaist makers' local, number 25, created in 1905, whereas the better-skilled male tailors, cutters, and pressers belonged to Local 10. This structure automatically created gender discrimination.

A majority of the membership of the ILGWU was Jewish, but other ethnic minorities, such as Italians, were represented. Although the union newspaper came out in three languages— English, Yiddish, and Italian—some members complained that they could not participate in debates, most of which took place in Yiddish. Yiddish was indeed the predominant language, and it appears that Jewish immigrants had most of the responsibilities.

Concerned with social justice, the Jewish unions, including the ILGWU, disagreed with the "apolitical" corporatist and anti-immigration tendencies of the labor aristocrats of the AFL.[26] But, in fact, the beliefs of the Jewish unions and of the AFL were not mutually exclusive. John Dyche, long-time secretary of the ILGWU, was a moderate and, like Samuel Gompers, president of the AFL, did not believe in the effectiveness of frequent strikes.[27]

As Irving Howe notes, "For girls in the immigrant Jewish neighborhoods, there were special problems. . . . Both American and Jewish expectations pointed in a single direction—marriage and motherhood. But the position of the Jewish woman

---

26. Menes, "The East Side and the Jewish Labor Movement," 215–16.
27. Howe, *World of Our Fathers*, 296.

was rendered anomalous by the fact that, somehow, the Jewish tradition enforced a combination of social inferiority and business activity."[28] In the bildungsroman *Bread Givers,* Anzia Yezierska, a Russian-Jewish immigrant, comments on this divided identity. Sarah, the heroine, is perpetually torn between conflicting ways of life, both equally harsh and mutilating: on the one hand, excruciatingly hard work and loneliness leading to personal achievement and freedom; on the other, a sheltered but suffocating life at home under the crushing weight of religious and patriarchal tyranny. Yezierska shows how intellectual and emotional progress leads her heroine to reconcile these two conflicts. Integrating education and work with a family life in which there is an awareness of tradition and roots is the only way to achieve maturity, fulfillment, and "Americanization" (and remain "a mensch"). Sarah's solution may sound trite to us now, but both Howe and Yezierska addressed crucial questions about the gender roles of first- and second-generation immigrant Jewish women.

Most Jewish immigrant women had backgrounds in agriculture or small-scale industrial production. In either case the squalid urban and industrial society they confronted in the New World undermined their traditional notions of womanhood. At the same time, having engaged in economic activities in Eastern Europe, even if they were subservient, helped the women adapt to the melting pot. The old country's culture and the New World's goals, as Elizabeth Ewen argues, were connected in a dynamic process.[29]

In the *shtetl,* women had been excluded from study and ritual by their religion and by patriarchy. While enforcing their inferior status, this situation had nevertheless enabled them to ful-

28. Ibid., 265.
29. Ewen, *Immigrant Women,* preface.

fill a significant domestic role inside and outside the home. While the men studied, the women peddled and ran small businesses. Thus, in spite of gender discrimination and misogyny, the women not only worked outside the home, they also prepared to work in America.[30] Ewen found, for example, that some garment workers had already learned their crafts in their home countries of Italy, Galicia, and Poland.[31]

Although the Jewish woman normally stopped working for wages once she married, earning money was part of her life.[32] In 1913, Alice Kessler-Harris notes, women represented 70 percent or more of the workers in the dress and waist industry. Many of those who were unmarried sent part of their earnings back home, and, married or unmarried, almost 90 percent in New York City turned all of their wages over to their families.[33]

Despite the tension between the cultural prescription of domesticity and economic necessity, the working woman was a "central cultural figure" in Yiddish socialist literature.[34] In real life, however, working women, such as those in the shirtwaist trade, had extremely hard lives.

Work in the Shirtwaist Trade   Ethnic variety characterized the work force of the garment industry. In the shirtwaist trade, Russian Jews represented 55 percent of the female work force; Italians, 35 percent; and native-born Americans, 7 percent.[35] Quoting a Women's Trade Union League leader, Helen Marot, Meredith Tax notes that 70 percent of the 1909–10 strikers were

30. Robinson, "Daughters of the Shtetl."

31. Ewen, *Immigrant Women,* 244–45.

32. Kessler-Harris,"Organizing the Unorganizable," 6.

33. Kessler-Harris, *Out to Work,* 126.

34. Schofield, "The Uprising of the 20,000," 179; Buhle, *Women and American Socialism,* 178.

35. Kessler-Harris, "Organizing the Unorganizable," 6.

Russian-Jewish women, 20 percent Russian-Jewish men, 6 percent Italian women, and 3 percent native-born women. Russian Jews thus represented 90 percent of the strikers.[36]

A contemporary article conveys the feverish atmosphere in which the shirtwaist makers worked:

> Mounting the stairs of the waist factory, one is aware of heavy vibrations. The roar and whir of the machines increases as the door opens, and one sees in a long loft . . . rows and rows of girls with heads bent and eyes intent on the flashing needles. They are all intensely absorbed; for if they be paid by the piece they hurry from ambition, and if they be paid by the week they are "speeded up" by the foreman to a pace set by the swiftest workers.[37]

Commenting on the mixture of familiarity and harassment, Pauline Newman reported on her own experience in the Triangle factory at the age of nine or ten:

> I worked on the 9th floor with a lot of youngsters like myself. . . . When the operators were through with sewing shirtwaists, there was a little thread left, and we youngsters would get a little scissors and trim the threads off. And when the inspectors came around, do you know what happened? The supervisors made all the children climb into one of those crates . . . and they covered us over with finished shirtwaists . . . because, of course, we were too young to be working in the factory legally. The Triangle Waist Company was a family affair, all relatives of the owner running the place, watching you. . . . And if you were two or three minutes longer [in the toilet] than foremen or foreladies thought you should be, it was deducted from your pay. . . . Rubber heels came into use around that time and our employers were the first to use them; you never knew when they would sneak up on you, spying, to be sure you did not talk to each other during work hours.[38]

---

36. Tax, *Rising of the Women*, 211.
37. Clark and Wyatt, "Working-Girls' Budgets," 72.
38. Quoted in Wertheimer, *We Were There*, 294.

How widespread were these working conditions? By 1900, there were about five hundred "shops" employing eighteen thousand women.[39] In 1910, Sue A. Clark and Edith Wyatt described "factories," as the larger shops were called, that employed four hundred to five hundred women. There were also hundreds of small shops that employed five to twenty women. Because the shirtwaist trade had appeared fairly recently, the workshops, most of them north of Fourteenth Street, were more salubrious and more modern than those in most other sectors of the garment trade. Nonetheless, conditions were deplorable. The workday was usually from 8:00 A.M. to 6:30 P.M. with thirty minutes for lunch, for a total of fifty-six hours a week.[40] In the busy season, women often worked for up to seventy hours a week without any pay for overtime.[41]

Because the trade was subject to the whims of fashion and to the subcontracting system, the distribution of work and pay varied wildly throughout the year. The seasonal rhythm, with peaks in the spring and fall and four- to eight-week periods when no work was available, made year-long employment practically impossible. Unemployment and precariousness were thus part of everyday life. Clark and Wyatt describe one woman's plight: "Out of the twelve months of the year, for one month she was idle, for four months she had only three or four days' work a week and for four months only did she have work for all six days. Unhappily during these months she developed a severe cough, which lost her seven weeks of work, and gave her . . . the expense of medicine, a doctor."[42]

Manufacturing processes also varied wildly. In some firms, one worker would sew a whole shirtwaist. Elsewhere, the work was endlessly subdivided, from the skilled and relatively well-

---

39. Buhle, *Women and American Socialism,* 184.
40. Clark and Wyatt, "Working-Girls' Budgets," 71.
41. Goodman and Weland, "The Shirtwaist Trade," 819.
42. Clark and Wyatt, "Working-Girls' Budgets," 72.

paid designer to the finishers, often children, who trimmed and cut excess thread from the garments or the sewing machines. In between were the cutters (always well-paid men), the sewing machine operators (usually women), the ironers, and others. The pay varied according to skill and workplace and, therefore, gender. At the bottom of the scale were the apprentices and finishers, who made three or four dollars a week. The "aristocrats"—designers, drapers, and sample makers, as well as cutters and pressers, almost all of whom were men—earned twelve to sixteen dollars.[43] The machine operators (50 to 60 percent of the work force) earned from eight to thirteen dollars a week. For the majority of women in the trade, the pay was extremely inadequate. A study of the shirtwaist worker's budget shows that such wages could not possibly cover the basic outlays for food, lodging, and medical bills.[44]

A double wage system added to the confusion and arbitrariness. Workers were paid by the week or by the piece. The Eastern European and Italian workers Ewen interviewed seemed to hate the week system because it made them into slaves and turned foremen and foreladies into slave drivers. They found piecework more relaxed and human because it allowed for social exchange at work. Some women observed, however, that pieceworkers tended to drive themselves to produce and to become their own oppressors.[45]

Derived from kinship ties and patterns of upward mobility, that is, the features of immigration, the subcontracting system contributed to the built-in inequality of wages, particularly between men and women. According to *The Souvenir History of the Strike*, subcontracting evolved because of the lack of managerial experience of the "proprietors," who had only recently been promoted from worker status to that of employers: "This is

43. Interview, Sonia Farber, August 1979.
44. Clark and Wyatt, "Working-Girls' Budgets," 72.
45. Ewen, *Immigrant Women*, 248.

16

how . . . they [the proprietors] called in a workman and made a contract with him. . . . They rented or loaned him the machines and encouraged him to get as much work out of a young girl for as little money as he could. . . . By this means the girls' bosses were doubled . . . and two profits to one were taken out of her labor."[46] During the busy season subcontractors would take on assembly work from larger firms or a foreman and hire women, apprentices for the most part, for the lowest possible price to assemble the pieces. The work was performed "inside" (i.e., in the factory) or "outside" (i.e., in the home), which encouraged the hiring of children and married women.[47] The union estimated that 37 percent of the learners in the trade—girls who made from $2.50 to $4.00 a week—worked for subcontractors. This system reinforced the sexual division of labor and gender inequality in the workplace.[48]

Exploitation of the women based on class, gender, and ethnicity was most manifest in their excessively long workdays and pathetically low wages. But it was reinforced more subtly. Besides earning a pittance, the women were subject to a harsh system of fines, including, for instance, for being five minutes late in the morning. They also had to pay for the electricity to run their machines, with a profit to the employer, and for each needle they broke. And they had to rent their chairs and pay twenty-five cents to store their hats in a locker. Employers also would pair a Russian Jew with an Italian or a girl earning eight dollars with one earning half as much, further increasing the workers' alienation. And, to exacerbate jealousy and ensure that workers did not communicate with one another, employers would "start stories to arouse race prejudice."[49]

Sexual discrimination also took the form of harassment, as

---

46. *Souvenir History*, 2–3.
47. Kessler-Harris, *Out to Work*, 150.
48. Tax, *Rising of the Women*, 210.
49. *Souvenir History*, 5.

union activist Clara Lemlich noted: "The bosses in the shops are hardly . . . educated men, and girls to them are part of the machines they are manning. They yell at the girls and they 'call them down' even worse than I imagine Negro slaves were in the South."[50]

Activist Rose Schneiderman tells a story that describes paradigmatically the relationships in the workshops between the young female workers and the older male employers, who in some cases were family: "Mr. Aptheker had a habit of pinching the girls whenever he passed them and they wanted it stopped. I went to see him, and . . . told him . . . that the girls resented it, and would he please stop it. . . . Looking at me in great amazement, he said 'Why, Miss Schneiderman, these girls are like my children!' Without a blink, one woman answered 'Mr. Aptheker, we would rather be orphans.' "[51] In this case, a worker had the courage and skill to challenge the infantilization. More often, like a young Russian woman who wrote to the *Jewish Daily Forward* in 1907, women were sexually insulted and dismissed for resisting a foreman's advances. But in spite of the divisive practices and humiliation, or because of it, the women developed a sense of solidarity, of "camaraderie," that cut across their ethnic differences and inequality of pay. One of Ewen's respondents talks of "a clear distinction between the bosses, the male workers and the women workers. The bosses kept their distance, the male cutters made sexual comments, but the women got along well together."[52] They even celebrated each other's weddings.

Women and Trade Unions

Female sewing machine operators employed in the shirtwaist industry led the series of strikes that breathed life into the mori-

50. Lemlich, "Why Waistmakers Strike."
51. Schneiderman, *All for One*, 86–87.
52. Ewen, *Immigrant Women*, 250.

bund International Ladies' Garment Workers' Union between 1909 and 1911.[53]

Founded in 1906, Local 25 of the ILGWU, the shirtwaist makers' union, saw its membership increase in 1909 from one hundred to eight hundred, and by 1910, it had twenty thousand members. Yet the proportion of women workers in trade unions in general remained low. Around 1900, only 3.3 percent of the women engaged in industrial occupations were organized. By 1920, the figure was still only 6.6 percent, and half of them were in the clothing trade.[54]

Writing on this reluctance to organize, Meredith Tax concludes: "Women were unorganized because they were docile, easily managed and cheap because they were unorganized. In fact they were unorganized because they had just become workers . . . because their husbands, boyfriends and fathers did not let them go to meetings."[55] All of this points to a vicious cycle. Domestic and industrial factors worked in tandem. Because they changed their employment often, the women were badly paid, and because their pay was low and their jobs unstable, they had little energy to devote to organizing.

Australian labor journalist Alice Henry noted in 1915 that the indifference and youthful arrogance of the young workers contributed to their reluctance to organize.[56] At the turn of the century, 87 percent of female workers were unmarried, and nearly half were under twenty-five. The most powerful motivator in their lives was the expectation of marriage. Even if young Jewish girls worked outside the home, they expected to marry and leave the work force. Engaging in union activity did not enhance their chances.[57] Rose Schneiderman's mother, for exam-

53. Kessler-Harris, *Out to Work*, 150.
54. Ibid., 152.
55. Tax, *Rising of the Women*, 32.
56. Henry, *Trade Union Woman*, 146.
57. Kessler-Harris, *Out to Work*, 159.

ple, warned her daughter against such involvement: "She kept saying I'd never get married because I was so busy—a prophecy which came true."[58] The Lower East Side may have approved of the working girl's image, but marriage remained the symbol of the traditional female role.

Both the AFL and the UHT, far from enrolling women in the common struggle, tended to exclude them. While half-heartedly trying to unionize young women, they subscribed to the patriarchal dogma that married women should stay home and not work. This dated discourse often concealed a fear on the part of AFL leaders, for example, of competition from women.[59]

"Many labor men are men first and unionists second," wrote Helen Marot, an active Quaker member of the Women's Trade Union League.[60] One incident after another illustrates the unions' reluctance to organize women, which sometimes led to discrimination against women unionists. Pauline Newman, one of the first female ILGWU officials, left the union, for which she had been organizing in Cleveland, because it paid her less than it did male organizers.[61] And in 1904, when Rose Schneiderman, then a young worker in a cap makers' firm, decided with a few others to join a union, they were told that twenty-five prospective members were required for their request to be accepted.[62]

Not surprisingly, women were excluded from positions of responsibility at all levels. Helen Marot noted that out of 111 national trade unions, only 1 had a woman president.[63] And in

---

58. Schneiderman, *All for One,* 50. Kessler-Harris notes that "the moment she organizes a union and seeks by organization to secure better wages, she diminishes or destroys what is to the employer her chief value" (*Out to Work,* 153).

59. Kessler-Harris, *Out to Work,* 153.

60. Marot, *American Labor Unions,* 72.

61. Kessler-Harris, "Organizing the Unorganizable," 15.

62. Schneiderman, *All for One.*

63. Marot, *American Labor Unions,* 76, 123.

the ILGWU, whose membership was two-thirds female, not one woman's name was mentioned in the minutes of the congresses before 1909. In Local 25, men held all union offices and eight of fifteen executive board positions, yet they represented a trade whose rank and file was 80 percent female.[64] At the rank-and-file level, union habits that conformed to the men's needs kept many women away: meetings took place late and in cafés; the men held forth on topics that did not always interest women; and no attention was paid to women's space, time, and occupations. Only leaders such as Rose Schneiderman, Pauline Newman, and Fania Cohn who had come up from the rank and file could confront the walls of hostility.

The situation did not change after the strikes. Antagonism or at best indifference from male workers persisted after 1910, although many women joined Local 25. Roger Waldinger illustrates several cases of resistance to unionization in the garment trade.

The poverty and cultural and linguistic diversity of the workers also slowed union organization considerably. In 1908, the Women's Trade Union League appointed Rose Schneiderman "organizer of the East Side." At first she shrank from the magnitude of the task, for when she urged the starving workers to organize, they answered that they would see about it once they found work. Schneiderman contented herself with informing the unions that the league could offer women instruction in English and union work.[65]

Attitudes toward unionization varied somewhat by ethnic group. Early on in their lives, the Russian-Jewish workers had overcome social and racial injustice. Radical and politically active, they protested spontaneously, even if, as Morris Hillquit complained, organizing did not come easily to them. Helen

---

64. Schofield, "The Uprising of the 20,000," 170.

65. WTUL report, 1908–9, Rose Schneiderman Papers, Box 2, Folder 6, Tamiment Library, New York University.

Marot, secretary of the WTUL, commented, "The Russian workers who filled New York factories are ever ready to rebel against the suggestion of oppression."[66] A 1908–9 WTUL report also acknowledged the women's dynamism: "The Jewish women are quick to organize, and the league has found in several trades that the membership of unions was wholly Jewish, while other nationalities working in the same trade were non-union."[67] The women tended to drop their efforts to organize, however, once a struggle was over and not to resist pressures for marriage and home.[68]

Italian women, who were more oppressed at home by family and church and less class conscious than the Jewish women, were apparently harder to organize, and it took a while to convince them not to desert the strike.[69] Of all the immigrants, they suffered the most from the language barrier and isolation. Yet, as Marot says, in 1911 the Italian women in Lawrence, Massachusetts, proved to be just as efficient at organizing as were the Jews in New York once enough attention was paid to their culture, language, and needs.[70]

As noted in Malkiel's *Diary,* American-born women were a nightmare to labor organizers. They displayed marked apathy, even hostility, to the strike. Their roots, connections, and language ability gave them an exaggerated sense of their privileged position in the labor world and blinded them to class oppression. Not surprisingly, the bosses tended to use them as strikebreakers. Marot observed that they wanted no unions and joined the strike, if they did at all, only out of philanthropic motives:

---

66. Marot, "A Woman's Strike," 222.
67. *Annual Report of the Women's Trade Union League, 1906–1909,* 7–8, WTUL Archives, New York State Labor Library, New York.
68. Waldinger, "Another Look at the ILGWU," 100.
69. Kessler-Harris, "Organizing the Unorganizable," 12.
70. Marot, "A Woman's Strike," 223.

"We have no grievance, we only struck in sympathy." It would have been strategically more effective, Marot notes, "if meetings had been left to the guidance of American men and women who understood their prejudices."[71] Pauline Newman boasted that she had managed to organize an English-speaking branch of the waist makers' union in Massachusetts, "and my dear not with eleven or twelve members—but with a good sturdy membership of forty."[72]

Most black women in turn-of-the-century New York were domestic workers. Excluded from factories, the few black women in the garment trade—only 803 were listed as dressmakers in New York—were outside the pale of organization, and during the strike black women were hired as scabs. The issue of prejudice against blacks was debated among white and black progressives, and finally black women were urged not to act as strikebreakers, even though they were excluded from Local 25 and sometimes from the shops. The league promised to organize women of color, but the effort was not to much avail before 1910.[73]

As this brief survey points out, for all their political and intellectual sophistication, Jewish women at the turn of the century lacked experience in industrial organization. Problems related to their status as immigrants and to their ethnicity, as well as class and gender conflicts, militated against mass protest. As I discuss in the next section, the groups of supporters who contributed energy, time, and money to the shirtwaist makers' strike—the Women's Trade Union League, women in the Socialist party, and suffragists—played a decisive part in helping the strikers overcome these obstacles.

---

71. Marot, "A Woman's Strike: An Appreciation of the Shirtwaist Makers," 189.

72. Quoted in Kessler-Harris, "Organizing the Unorganizable," 12.

73. Tax, *Rising of the Women,* 225–26.

The Uprising of the 20,000

Supporters of the Strike Before exploring the Uprising of the
20,000, I shall briefly discuss the organizations that supported
the shirtwaist makers' strike politically, logistically, and finan-
cially: the Women's Trade Union League, the suffragists, and
the Socialist Party of America.

The National Women's Trade Union League developed from a
commitment to relieve the social problems caused by the rapid
industrialization occurring in the United States. Driven by hu-
manitarian motives but also by a need to escape the depressing
idleness of their daily lives, women from well-to-do families,
"the Social housekeepers" as they were called, transferred the
"female call" to self-sacrifice and the domestic mission into social action.[74]

When they confronted destitution, ignorance, overwork, and
underpay, however, the middle-class volunteers soon realized
that they should focus their energy on helping working women,
"their industrial sisters," organize. Gertrude Barnum, a league
member, underlined the futility of "introducing into their lives
books and flowers and music. . . . It did not raise their wages
or shorten their hours." With similar motivations, Lillian Wald,
a nurse on the East Side before she created the Henry Street
Settlement House, abruptly converted to the idea of trade
unionism.[75] Many settlement centers such as Hull House in
Chicago, Henry Street in New York, and Denison House in
Boston were used as the premises for organizing union locals.

Only a national organization could begin to deal with the
magnitude of the poverty problem. Thus, in 1903, philanthro-
pists met with male and female unionists, under the auspices of
the AFL, and founded the National Women's Trade Union

---

74. Dye, *As Equals and as Sisters*, 9.
75. Dreier in ibid., 1; Barnum in ibid., 41; Wald, *The House on Henry
Street*, 203.

League (WTUL). The first board was composed of two workers and two middle-class reformers.

Overall, the league's aims were to help women mobilize, to train organizers, to inform workers, and to sway public opinion in favor of unionism. In 1909, the league formulated specific short- and long-term goals: a shorter workday, equal pay for equal work regardless of sex or race, and the right of women to vote.[76]

From the beginning, the organization recruited among women workers, distributed propaganda, taught English and trade union principles, and held street meetings, which Helen Marot, among others, enjoyed unreservedly: "We had the best sort of time at them. . . . You just take a platform along, put up a banner and begin to talk. . . . Others go round and distribute circulars among the girls and ask questions. These circulars are in Yiddish, Italian and English and we vary them. . . . It gives tremendous courage to the union girls to have us talk there . . . I think these street meetings are something we can all get courage out of."[77]

Although the WTUL had largely middle-class origins, workers and "allies" (individuals outside the working class interested in unionizing women) worked together, not without tension, however. Who were the so-called "allies"? Helen Marot was a Quaker and a socialist who had been a secretary of the league since 1906. May and Margaret Dreier, who had joined in 1904, were the daughters of a German immigrant businessman and devout Lutheran. And Violet Pike and Carola Woerishoffer, young students from wealthy families, devoted themselves entirely to their underprivileged sisters. As a group, the "allies" were generally wealthy, well educated, and single, and many had experience in social reform or philanthropy.[78]

---

76. Pidgeon, *Toward Better Working Conditions for Women.*
77. Quoted in Wertheimer, *We Were There,* 273.
78. Dye, *As Equals and as Sisters,* 40.

Among the working-class immigrant women in the leadership of the league was Jewish activist Rose Schneiderman, who had arrived in the United States in 1891 at the age of nine and joined the league in 1905. A cap maker, she had an impressive background in industrial action and socialism and had encountered enough discrimination in unions to appreciate the league's initiatives.

Pauline Newman, another Russian-Jewish immigrant, joined the ILGWU and the league in 1909. Like Theresa Malkiel, she had been a member of the Socialist Party of America since 1906.[79] Newman wrote the following curriculum vita for herself for the June 1921 issue of *Life and Labor*: "College at the Triangle Waist Company at thirteen; M.A. from the ILGWU; . . . Ph.D. from the Women's Trade Union League in New York."[80] Never married, like Schneiderman, Newman was a full-time militant.

Leonora O'Reilly was one of the first recruits of the WTUL. Born into an Irish working-class family, she was a seamstress like her mother and grandmother. An outstanding orator, she joined the Socialist party in 1911 and actively took part in the shirtwaist makers' strike. Like Newman and Schneiderman, she supported women's suffrage.

Given the women's radically different social backgrounds, it is hardly surprising that class differences were obstacles to sisterhood and created problems in the WTUL. Leonora O'Reilly, for example, vehemently disapproved of the upper-class culture in the league: "Contact with the Lady does harm in the long run," she said. "It gives the wrong standard."[81] Pauline Newman likewise accused the "cultured ladies" of being ignorant of and indifferent to social conditions. Working women in the

---

79. In 1979, she regarded this as her most important political act. Interview, Pauline Newman, March 14, 1979.

80. Quoted in Neidle, *America's Immigrant Women*, 156.

81. Quoted in Dye, *As Equals and as Sisters*, 53.

league thus felt discriminated against both as underprivileged persons and as non-WASPS: "They don't understand the differences between Jewish girls and gentiles," Newman told Schneiderman.[82] The "allies" could not speak Yiddish and would schedule events on Jewish holidays, even on Yom Kippur. Furthermore, league literature indulged in stereotypical representations of the immigrant girls as "dark-eyed," "studious," "revolutionary" Jewish women and as "docile," "submissive," and "superstitious" Italians.[83]

Such tensions, according to Nancy Schrom Dye, prove that the league failed to integrate class and ethnicity and "to synthesize feminism with unionism," despite its recognition of the need for female solidarity and of the specific needs of working-class women.[84] In contrast, women in unions felt appreciated as members of the working class but denied as women. Thus, as Alice Kessler-Harris argues, women workers, whether they were socialists, immigrants, or members of other groups, were continually torn between class and gender consciousness. Nowhere were their multiple identities recognized.

The associations for women's suffrage—the Political Equality League of Self Supporting Women, the Woman's Suffrage party, and the National American Woman Suffrage Association (NAWSA)—gained momentum and membership around the time of the shirtwaist makers' strike. Nicknamed "high-society ladies" or "the mink brigade," most of the members of these groups came from the middle and upper classes.[85] Alva Belmont (1853–1953), who had been married to W. K. Vanderbilt and belonged to one of the four hundred richest families in New York (the "four hundreds"), was president of the Po-

---

82. Quoted in Kessler-Harris, "Organizing the Unorganizable," 12.
83. Dye, *As Equals and as Sisters*, 54.
84. Ibid., 4.
85. Schneiderman, *All for One*, 8.

litical Equality League at the time of the strike. Her support of the strikers and that of other prominent socialites arose from a commitment to the vote for women and took the form of large financial contributions and fund-raising events, such as a huge meeting on December 5, 1909, and the "motorcade" of December 21.

Although some socialites belonged to the WTUL, the labor unions and associations were generally ambivalent, not to say hostile, to the presence and interference of the millionairesses in the strike. Malkiel remarks in *The Diary of a Shirtwaist Striker* that the thousand dollars collected at the Colony Club was only a minute sacrifice for such wealthy ladies. The January 10, 1910, issue of the anarchist newspaper *Solidarity* denounced the women's motivations as lust for fame, adventure, and prominence. In the eyes of socialists, the socialites' one-sided interest in the strikers as potential voters, regardless of their class situation, could only weaken the working women's revolutionary fiber. Unbridgeable differences between the "girls" and the "society ladies," as well as the latter's political manipulations, were pervasive during this period.

Speaking at a meeting on December 12, 1909, labor activist Emma Goldman expressed her distrust of suffrage politics. High-society suffragists, she argued, thought of their cause as identical with that of working women, but once they obtained the vote, she predicted, they would consider only their own class interests.[86] As an anarchist and thus someone who dismissed reformism, Goldman could see through the opportunistic motives of many such groups.

While league members and suffragists supported the shirtwaist makers' strike largely out of solidarity, women in the Socialist party regarded the strike as a major political event and

---

86. *New York World,* December 13, 1909.

made it their special responsibility. Elected on December 19, 1909, a committee of twelve Socialist party women organized support for the strikers in close collaboration with the WTUL. An article in the *New York Call* on February 8, signed by Theresa Malkiel and two socialist activists, Meta Stern and Antoinette Konikow, summarized the committee members' roles as those of organizers, secretaries, members of strike pickets, newspaper sellers, sandwich women, and fund raisers.

The Socialists' political goals were first to support the strikers' short-term aims, set by the ILGWU. Over the long term, they demanded union power (i.e., the closed shop) and advocated use of a single contract for the industry instead of the union's short-sighted tactic of separate agreements for each local.[87]

Although they overlapped some in their views on the strike, the suffragists focused primarily on the women's vote and the women Socialists on the class struggle. The WTUL with its dominant middle-class membership but influential socialist activists reached in more directions. They believed in solidarity between women, but they also fought against the oppression of women/workers/immigrants. Among the supportive organizations, the league came nearest to integrating issues of class and gender.

The Strike

In the black of winter of nineteen-nine
When we froze and bled on the picket line,
We showed the world that women could fight
And we rose and won with women's might.

---

87. They also protested the considerable differences in wages among union delegates—fifteen to eighteen dollars a week—and strike allowances, which never exceeded two dollars.

Hail the waistmakers of nineteen-nine
Making their stand on the picket line,
Breaking the power of those who reign,
Pointing the way, smashing the chain.

—"The Uprising of the 20,000"[88]

Beginning in August 1909, spontaneous strikes and walkouts frequently disrupted the shirtwaist industry. The workers' demands concerned working conditions, pay, and union rights. The employers—Louis Leiserson, Rosen Brothers, and the Triangle Waist Company—retaliated immediately by calling in the police and hiring scabs, thugs, and prostitutes to beat up the picketers.

As the labor leaders began to think of calling a general strike, signs of support began to emerge. The membership of Local 25 of the ILGWU, which was only one hundred in 1909, started to increase.[89] At a meeting on October 21, members of the local spoke in favor of the strike and demanded a wage increase of 10 percent, union recognition, and an end to the police brutality.[90] And on October 28, the cutters, organized separately in Local 3, decided to support their "organized sisters."[91]

As the idea of the strike gathered momentum, a legendary meeting took place on November 22 at Cooper Union. While union officials, socialist lawyers, and members of the WTUL sat on the platform, young women workers in billowing hats and shirtwaists filled the hall. For two hours, speeches were presented in Yiddish and English, summing up the situation, preaching moderation, and begging the "girls" to stick to their unions until their demands were satisfied.[92]

88. Quoted in Wertheimer, *We Were There,* 293.
89. Levine, *Women Garment Workers,* 122, 151.
90. *New York Call,* October 22, 1909.
91. *Souvenir History,* 8.
92. Levine, *Women Garment Workers,* 154.

At this point, Clara Lemlich, a young woman employed at Leiserson's, who had already been beaten up and arrested seventeen times, leaped onto the platform, interrupting the bureaucratic drone. Within minutes she had aroused the apathetic crowd:[93]

> Making her way to the platform, she delivered a "phillipic" in Yiddish: "I am a working girl, one of those who are on strike against intolerable conditions. I am tired of listening to speakers. . . . What we are here for is to decide whether we shall or shall not strike. I offer a resolution that a general strike shall be declared— now." Instantly, the big gathering was on its feet, everyone shouting an emphatic affirmative, waving hats, canes, handkerchiefs. . . . For five minutes perhaps the tumult continued; when the chairman could make himself heard, he asked for a seconder of the resolution. Again, the big audience leapt to their feet, everyone seconding.[94]

The Souvenir History of the Strike tells us that "the chairman then cried, 'Do you mean faith? Will you take the old Jewish oath?' and up came two thousand right hands, with the prayer, 'If I turn traitor to the cause I now pledge, may this hand wither away from the arm I now raise,' and thus started this historic general strike, probably the greatest struggle for unionism among women the world has ever seen."[95]

Once the decision was made, the strike surged like a tidal wave through the Lower East Side.[96] By ten o'clock the next morning, according to the *Souvenir History,* "15,000 working women had stopped work." Journalist Alice Henry wrote: "From every waist-making factory, the girls poured forth, filling the narrow streets of the East Side, crowding the headquar-

---

93. Clara Lemlich, an immigrant from the Ukraine, was a skilled draper and union organizer. A founder of Local 25, she had led the walkout in Leiserson's shop and been beaten up while picketing.

94. Levine, *Women Garment Workers,* 154.

95. *Souvenir History,* 12.

96. *New Yorker Volkszeitung,* December 9, 1909.

ters at Clinton Hall, and overflowing into twenty-four smaller halls in the vicinity. It was like a mighty army, rising in the night, and demanding to be heard."[97]

Everywhere, work came to a stop. In the unionized workshops, one worker (male or female) blew a whistle to give the signal.[98] More often, confusion reigned. In many shops, the girls sat down in their usual places but kept their coats on and did not move: "We stayed whispering, and no one knowing what the other would do, not making up our minds for two hours. . . . We hardly knew where to go—or what to do next. But one of the American girls who knew how to telephone, called up the Women's Trade Union League, and they told us all to come to a big hall a few blocks away."[99]

The strikers poured into the union building by the hundreds. Organizing this "undisciplined army" presented a serious challenge. Within the first hours, Local 25 enrolled the strikers and arranged for their subsistence and for their protection from the police and the employers' thugs. At this point the staff of the WTUL went into action—Margaret Dreier, the president; Leonora O'Reilly, the vice-president; Helen Marot, the secretary-general; and Rose Schneiderman, the organizer for the East Side, who stated their aim: "to arouse public sympathy, appeal against police outrages and work side by side with the strikers."[100]

Three committees, one formed by the Socialist party, one by the UHT, and another by the Italian branch of the Socialist party, along with many volunteers, rented rooms all over the Lower East Side; found English-, Italian-, and Yiddish-language speakers; organized the strikers by shops and linguis-

97. Henry, *Trade Union Woman*, 93.

98. *Souvenir History*, 8.

99. Clark and Wyatt, "Working-Girls' Budgets," 81.

100. Schneiderman, "The League Goes into Action," 6 (unpublished manuscript).

tic groups; formed picket lines; planned tactics against bosses, strikebreakers, and police; and helped each shop elect a delegate and formulate its demands. Fairly rapidly, order grew out of confusion. Members of the WTUL assisted union officials; sponsored an information bureau at Clinton Hall, the union headquarters; and responded to requests for speakers.

The strikers were then distributed to about twenty halls where meetings took place day and night. The members of the union executive committee almost never went to bed. The author of the *Souvenir History* evokes the long nights spent standing or sitting on chairs at the headquarters, the hurriedly eaten sandwiches, and the harassing conditions.[101]

In the short term, the workers demanded better working conditions and salaries, the abolition of the subcontracting system and of fines, a fifty-two-hour week, weekly pay, the limitation of overtime to three evenings a week of less than two hours, an equal distribution of work during the slack season, and payment for supplies (thread, needles, and electricity). Wages were to be negotiated in each firm.

The long-term objective was union recognition, which overlapped with the issue of "closed shop" (i.e., union control over hiring and working conditions). Union recognition would remain a priority and the symbol of the employers' resistance throughout the strike.[102]

Determined to break the strike, the employers (the thirty or forty large companies), organized as the Association of Waist and Dress Manufacturers, declared war against the unionists in the name of the "freedom to work" and persisted in hiring without consideration of union membership. These companies used newly arrived immigrants and black workers as strikebreakers.

---

101. *Souvenir History,* 14.
102. Goodman and Weland, "The Shirtwaist Trade," 816.

Others closed their factories in New York and reopened in the suburbs. Above all, they subcontracted part of their merchandise to smaller companies. [103]

Unable to survive, the small shops entered into negotiations right away. "Fifty-one bosses settled with the unions and hundreds of girls return to work to day," a reporter wrote in the *New York Call* on November 25, 1909. Four months after the beginning of the strike, more than one-third of the strikers (10,500 out of 30,000) had resumed work. [104] The ability of the large shops to subcontract work had undermined the collective and economic base of the strike and hence its victory.

After a spectacular start, the strike dragged on "from a pleasant late autumn to a miserable mid-winter." [105] Throughout these bitter months, the picket lines were the scene of daily struggle and confrontation. Hundreds of "girls," thinly clad and weakened by hunger, spent hours tramping the street in the mud and snow, challenging the employers' determination to reestablish the "freedom to work," defying police, strikebreakers, bodyguards, and prostitutes. Frequently, fights broke out on the picket lines. Women from the league displayed great vigilance, spotting strikebreakers, keeping an eye on the police, and occasionally standing on the lines.

As the strike wore on, the women faced the constant threat of arrest as police harassment increased. On December 25, 1909, the *New York Call* listed 738 strikers arrested to date, 19 of whom had been sent to the workhouse on Blackwell's Island. Strikers sentenced to a few days there were treated like ordinary criminals. Wearing a uniform made of "very heavy, coarse material, with stripes all around," the strikers worked for hours at menial tasks. [106] According to contemporary sources, the women

103. *New York World,* December 30, 1909.
104. Tax, *Rising of the Women,* 227.
105. Dubofsky, *When Workers Organize,* 52.
106. Clark and Wyatt, "Working-Girls' Budgets," 83.

met these ordeals stoically. Morris Hillquit remarked, "Jail has no terror for girls who have been confined for years in workshops that are worse than a prison."[107]

Fines totaled $1,296,000. The league proved extraordinarily efficient in providing the strikers with legal assistance by finding lawyers and arranging for bail. *The Souvenir History of the Strike* lists an impressive array of lawyers who assisted the defendants in court and established a chart of the rights and duties of strike pickets.[108]

Undeterred, the women fought on. Sympathetic witnesses and newspapers, especially the *New York Call,* reported on the struggle and mistreatment of the strikers. Louis Levine mentions a Miss Reisen, in charge of Italian workers, who not only convinced the reluctant ones to stay away from the shops but had learned enough Italian "to win the hearts of the Italian strikers." Esther Lobetkine, recently arrived from Russia, never left her group of strikers for a second: she would grab a little sleep, a sandwich; that was enough.[109]

The strike experience changed the activists profoundly and made ordinary women into heroines and adolescents into adults. A woman journalist from *Collier's* magazine, for example, marvelled at the joyful atmosphere at the union's headquarters and the maturity of a fifteen-year-old who explained the workers' demands to her. "From the Ghetto coquette the child passed in the twinkling of an eye into an orator," the journalist commented.[110]

The strikers were hailed as superwomen and symbols of feminine abnegation. John Dyche, president of the ILGWU, declared: "Here the fact was demonstrated again that women are better warriors than men. They have shown exemplary loyalty,

---

107. *New York Call,* January 3, 1910.
108. *Souvenir History,* 22, 27.
109. Levine, *Women Garment Workers,* 156–57.
110. *Collier's,* December 25, 1909.

devotion and self-sacrifice. Neither the police, nor the hooligan hirelings of the bosses, nor the biting frost and chilling snow of December and January damped their willingness to picket the shops from early morn till late at night."[111] The very men who had ignored or discriminated against the women lavished hyperboles.

While the strikers played their part as heroines, the supporters continued to work tirelessly, writing propaganda, collecting funds for the payment of fines, legal costs, bail, and strike allowance, and organizing demonstrations. Women from the league tapped their many resources: women's clubs, wealthy colleges on the East Coast, and members of the "four hundreds."

Union members and socialists sent out their most militant men and women to collect money. Pauline Newman in Buffalo and in New England and Rose Schneiderman in Boston were very effective fund raisers. The executive committee of the New York Socialist party gave $50,000 to the strike fund. The employees of the Knickerbocker Company collected $300 at a dance. The Federation of Manhattan Musicians Union gave a concert and raised $100. Vassar College women collected over $100 at a meeting held in sympathy for "their sisters that toil and are forced to strike."[112] Both the energy displayed to get financial support and the results were extraordinary.

All through these months, the ILGWU and its supporters organized meetings and demonstrations where they harangued the troops, celebrated the strikers, assessed the situation, and outlined political strategy. On December 3, 1909, the Socialist party sponsored the first mass meeting following the Cooper Union rally on November 22. The *Souvenir History* noted Theresa Malkiel's speech and her efficiency in organizing the subsequent parade to City Hall, "a monster indignation parade,

111. *Ladies' Garment Worker,* May 1910, 2.
112. *Souvenir History,* 17, 24.

10,000 striking Waist Makers, marching four abreast . . . to call upon the Mayor, their Mayor, to present to him their petition and their protests against the abuse and mistreatment received at the hands of their police force."[113] A rare harmony was displayed that day between strike supporters. Socialists, WTUL members prominent in the parade, and Mrs. Belmont's Political and Equality League all organized meetings that day.

Following these meetings, on December 5, the Political and Equality League organized "one of the largest meetings in the history of organized labor" in the Hippodrome, which they rented for the union. "In the boxes were many fashionable people," and on the mammoth stage, union and political leaders presented their views of the strike situation. The *New York Call* reported that "the audience was representative of all classes and organizations. There were suffragists, labormen, socialists and even some of the wealthy classes."[114]

Leonora O'Reilly pleaded the women's cause. Socialist Rose Pastor Stokes evoked the conflicting class interests and encouraged the striking girls to get a political education and to read Karl Marx: "I bring to you the message from forty million men and women, working men and women from the world over, and this message is: 'Workers of the world unite! You have nothing to lose but your chains.' "[115] Suffragist Anna Howard Shaw argued that all women, whatever their class, must demand the vote.

On December 9, the New York Socialists held a large meeting at the Thalia Theatre. Mother Jones, the guest speaker, aroused wild enthusiasm by telling the audience that "every strike she had been in was won by the women."[116]

---

113. Ibid., 14.
114. *New York Call*, December 6, 1909.
115. Ibid.
116. *New York Call*, December 10, 1909.

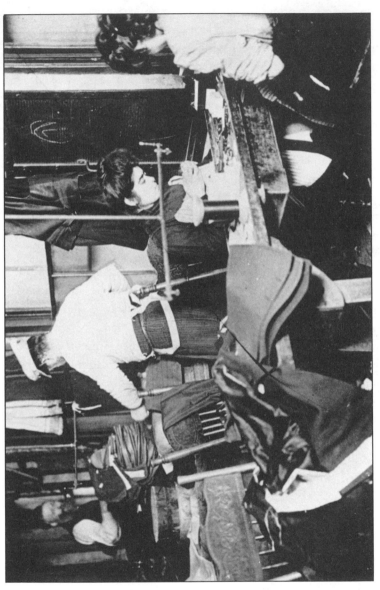

The workplace: a small garment shop (International Ladies' Garment Workers' Union Archives, Labor-Management Documentation Center, Cornell University)

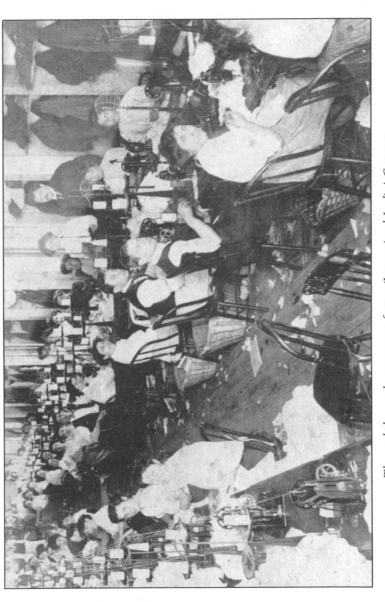

The workplace: a large garment factory (International Ladies' Garment Workers' Union Archives, Labor-Management Documentation Center, Cornell University)

The community: a Jewish tenement district (International Ladies' Garment Workers' Union Archives, Labor-Management Documentation Center, Cornell University)

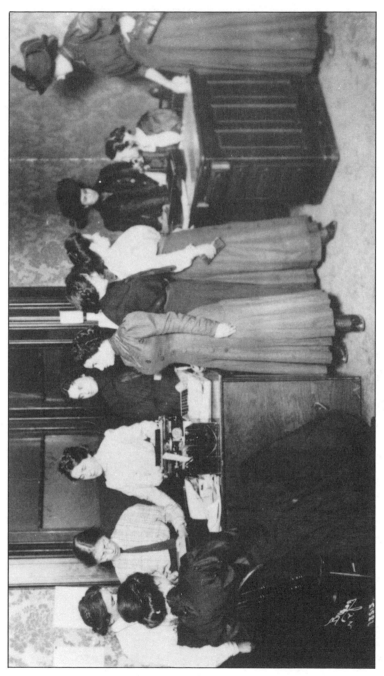

*The shirtwaist strike: headquarters of the WTUL, 43 East 22nd Street,
New York, January 1910 (Byron Collection, Museum of the City of New York)*

The shirtwaist strike: volunteering for picket duty at strike headquarters

(International Ladies' Garment Workers' Union Archives, Labor-Management Documentation Center, Cornell University)

The shirtwaist strike: strikers selling the special strike edition of the New York Call, December 29, 1909 (International Ladies' Garment Workers' Union Archives, Labor-Management Documentation Center, Cornell University)

Four days later, thousands gathered to hear the results of ongoing negotiations between the union and manufacturers: 236 firms had settled. But the results were inconclusive.

The wealthy members of suffragist societies chose a different style of support. On December 16, a committee of society ladies took ten of the "girl strikers" to lunch at the exclusive Colony Club. The idea was to acquaint the very rich with the very poor. A *New York Call* journalist reported:

> These women . . . had come to listen to the story of the strikers told in simple words by those who had been mistreated, abused, enslaved by capitalism, poverty and police persecution. Four hundred women, representing the richest people of the world, occupied as many gilt chairs in the beautiful gymnasium of the sumptuous club. In contradiction to this bejeweled, befurred, belaced, begowned audience, Miss Mary E. Dreier, President of the Women's Trade Union League, brought with her ten of the girl strikers . . . . some of them mere children.[117]

Clara Lemlich and Rose Schneiderman were among the speakers. The event raised one thousand dollars for the strikers, but it shocked many people in the labor world who found the suffragists' performance voyeuristic and in poor taste.

On December 21, the same suffragists organized a motorcade along Fifth Avenue with banners and posters, "a novel sight" indeed. In the sumptuous cars, the working girls sat next to the rich women. The mainstream press, naturally, made much of the sensational contrast between wealth and poverty, youth and middle age, and reveled in sentiment and stereotypes. The labor press made sarcastic remarks.[118]

The lavish style of these two events contrasted sharply with that of the socialists, who sent a delegation to the ferry pier on December 20 to meet a group of girls returning from

---

117. *New York Call*, December 22, 1909.
118. Ibid.

the Blackwell's Island workhouse. Two days later, an evening of music, poetry, and awards, followed by a ball, was held in their honor. Featured was a vocal performance by Miss Mulholland, who had once led the audience in singing the "Marseillaise."[119]

On December 27, the negotiators convened the strikers in five halls to inform them of the employers' proposal: a fifty-hour week, no discrimination against union members, four paid holidays a year, and negotiations about wages. Union recognition had not been granted.[120] The proposal was rejected unanimously. "We will be hungry unionists rather than well-fed scabs," the women responded.[121] On through January and February, the crucial issue of union recognition would deadlock negotiations.

On December 29 and 30, the *New York Call* printed a special edition of the paper in English, Italian, and Yiddish in which it told the story of the strike. Posted at strategic points, and wearing white sashes, the strikers sold the paper for five cents a copy or at "the buyer's generosity." The sale was a resounding success, and the proceeds were donated to the union.

The last large meeting took place on January 2, 1910, in Carnegie Hall and was organized by the league, the Socialist party, and other groups to protest police brutalities and to pay homage to the arrested strikers. In front of the platform sat 20 women who had been sent to Blackwell's Island and behind them on the stage 350 strikers wearing white sashes with the inscription "Arrested" or "Workhouse prisoner." "Hearty applause greeted twelve of the women Socialist Committee when they dropped over the edge of their box a white silk banner worked in red."[122] Little Rose Perr, aged ten, was called to tes-

---

119. *Souvenir History,* 18.
120. Tax, *Rising of the Women,* 226.
121. *Souvenir History,* 19.
122. Ibid., 20.

tify on police brutality. With her braided hair and long dress, she moved the audience to tears. [123]

But in spite of the emotional impact of the meeting, the alliance between the socialist and liberal supporters of the strike was wearing thin. Leonora O'Reilly evoked the urgency of union rights and the legal right to picket. Then Morris Hillquit, in "the speech of the evening," according to *The Souvenir History of the Strike,* reminded the audience that the union alone was powerless to correct social injustice. These socialist messages so angered league member Anne Morgan that the next day in the press she accused O'Reilly and Hillquit of indoctrinating the young girls with fanatical socialist dogma. Hillquit and other socialists counterattacked by accusing Morgan of attempting to split supporters and strikers. [124] Anne Morgan promptly left the league and with the support of Eva Valesh, an AFL organizer, continued her campaign to discredit the league as a "socialist organization."

As the strike dragged on, foundering on union recognition, on which the Association of Waist and Dress Manufacturers refused to compromise, the political conflicts worsened, along with antisocialist manipulation. [125] Just as Alva Belmont and her wealthy friends had earlier tried to usurp the leadership of the strike, they now capitalized on the workers' demoralization. [126] Playing on the fear of "extremism," they persisted in trying to discredit the socialists, who they claimed had contributed propaganda to the strike and not much else. On behalf of the Woman's National Committee of the Socialist party, Malkiel, Stern, and Konikow wrote a strong article for the *New York Call,* protesting these slanderous statements, which arose, they claimed, from a fear of socialist influence among the strikers:

---

123. Ibid., 21–22.
124. *New York Call,* January 4, 1910.
125. *New York Call,* January 23, 1910.
126. *New York World,* December 22, 1909.

46

"The socialist women have become a power with the girls them-selves. No wonder Mr. Gompers raises his hands in alarm. The girls have found by experience who their friends are. They will not allow themselves to be fooled, as did the workmen."[127]

Meanwhile, ideological disputes and a sense of defeat spread among supporters as the employers continued steadfastly to resist union recognition. By mid-February, only 13 big com-panies were still on strike. According to the ILGWU, agree-ments had been made with 356 companies, 337 of which had adopted union conditions. And not only did the Association of Waist and Dress Manufacturers refuse to recognize the union, but some of the firms that had settled were breaking their agreements.[128] On February 15, 1910, the strike was de-clared over.

The events that followed the Uprising of the 20,000 point out both the strengths and weaknesses of the movement. The Triangle fire, for example, was a tragic consequence of its in-ability to enforce union recognition. A large firm, the Triangle Waist Company had refused to meet a demand for safe fire es-capes and open doors, and on March 25, 1911, the building went up in flames. Trapped inside, many girls jumped out win-dows to their deaths. Of 500 workers, 146 died, and many more were injured. Rose Schneiderman's speech after the trag-edy expressed deep anger over the general indifference expressed regarding the safety and lives of her co-workers: "Each week I must learn of the untimely deaths of my sister workers. . . . The life of men and women is so cheap and property is so sa-cred. There are so many for one job that it matters little if 143 [*sic*] of us are burned to death."[129]

127. "Socialist Women and the Shirtwaist Strike," *New York Call,* Febru-ary 8, 1910.

128. Goodman and Weland, "The Shirtwaist Trade," 816.

129. Quoted in Wertheimer, *We Were There,* 312.

Beyond the crucial issue of union recognition, it is not easy to assess the results of the strike. On the one hand, the workers undeniably achieved better working conditions, a pay increase, and an end to the subcontracting system. Further, the cloakmakers' strike in 1911 and the rise in unionization in the following years point to the influence of the shirtwaist strike on the growth of the labor movement. On the other hand, discrimination in skills and pay continued. In spite of the growing numbers of female members—by 1912, 50 percent of the ILGWU's 50,000 members were women—women were still excluded from responsible positions. Between 1910 and 1920, the New York City ILGWU locals elected 450 delegates to the six conventions held during that period; only 25 of the delegates were women.[130] The WTUL, the main defender of the equality of working women, left its mark on the ILGWU in the area of organizing and teaching. But despite its awareness that women lacked a voice and power in the union, the WTUL chose not to interfere with union policies.[131]

The unions were not alone in lacking a political perspective and a belief in gender equality. With its policy of nonintervention in union matters and its preoccupation with electoral issues, the Socialist party shared some of the responsibility.

One should perhaps look elsewhere for more positive impressions of the strike. For example, a union sympathizer noticed encouraging signs of solidarity and sisterhood: "I have observed many a Jewish girl with her arm around an Italian girl's neck, not able to speak one to the other, but both understanding they are fighting the same fight for each other's interest."[132] Just as the precarious alliance between socialists and suffragists was giving way, here and there solidarity between oppressed ethnic minorities was emerging.

---

130. Waldinger, "Another Look at the ILGWU," 99.
131. Hyman, "Labor Organizing and Female Institution Building," 38.
132. *Souvenir History,* 19.

Theresa Serber Malkiel (1874–1949)

T heresa Serber Malkiel belonged to a generation of Jewish female immigrants who dedicated themselves at the turn of the century to the labor movement and to socialism and later to suffragism. But unlike Clara Lemlich, Rose Schneiderman, Pauline Newman, and others whose papers are preserved in archives, we read little about Malkiel except in articles and pamphlets in the socialist press and in congress reports of the period. The scarcity of biographical information makes her one of "the many unsung Jewish militants."[133] In a biographical essay on Malkiel, Sally Miller notes that she is omitted from *The American Labor's Who's Who* and from *The Woman's Who Is Who in America.* Nor is she mentioned in *Notable American Women.*[134] Surprisingly, two of her contemporaries whom I interviewed in 1979, Pauline Newman and Sonia Farber, gave rather hazy explanations. I find this invisibility even more puzzling in that Malkiel emerges as a strong presence in Socialist party literature and in the shirtwaist strike.

The scanty biographical data on Malkiel include an article in the *Socialist Woman* in May 1909, brief and unsigned, that she probably wrote. Theresa Serber, according to the anonymous author, was born in Russia on May 1, 1874, in the small town of Bar, about 150 miles from Kiev. When racial laws expelled Jews from cities and barred them from universities and businesses, she emigrated, like many of her contemporaries. Arriving in New York in 1891, at the age of seventeen, she found work in the cloak-making trade. Within a year, she threw herself into labor and political battles. In 1892, she joined the Russian Workingmen's Club, and in 1894, she became active in unionizing her workplace. The Infant Cloakmakers' Union of New

---

133. Buhle, *Women and American Socialism,* 178.
134. Miller, "From Sweatshop Worker to Labor Leader." An exception is the *Encyclopedia of the American Left,* which includes an entry on Malkiel.

York joined the city's three major labor bodies—the declining Knights of Labor, the socialist Central Labor Federation, and the United Hebrew Trades. The union was short-lived, but its members, female Jewish radicals determined to fight exploitation and to organize, set a precedent for battles to come.[135]

Like many Jewish immigrants, Theresa Serber Malkiel brought a radical tradition to American labor and politics. She joined the Socialist Labor party (SLP) in 1893 and represented her union at the first convention of the party's labor federation, the Socialist Trade and Labor Alliance. But, like other prominent members of the SLP, Meyer London, Joseph Barondess, Abraham Cahan, and later Morris Hillquit, Malkiel tired of Daniel De Leon's sectarianism and dogmatism. In 1901, she joined the Social Democratic party, which merged with other groups to form the Socialist Party of America.[136]

In 1900, she married Leon A. Malkiel, who had emigrated to the United States in 1881. A daughter, Henrietta, was born in 1903. *Who's Who in America* reports that her husband was a New York lawyer who also dealt in real estate.[137] He belonged to the Socialist Labor party, the Socialist Party of America, and the Women's Trade Union League, and he held several positions as a judge. The family's moves from the Lower East Side to the Upper West Side of Manhattan and later to Westchester County are evidence of their upward mobility.

Marrying a businessman and a socialist comrade enabled Theresa Malkiel to escape the sweatshop. She did not drop out of the radical scene, however. Committed to her former co-workers, she remained passionately involved in socialist politics.

---

135. Buhle, *Women and American Socialism,* 176–78.

136. Miller, "From Sweatshop Worker to Labor Leader," 193.

137. The back page of one of Malkiel's socialist pamphlets, *Woman and Freedom*, contains the following advertisement: "Leon Malkiel: land for sale in the suburbs; 116 Nassau Street; plots and bungalows by the sea at a reasonable distance from New York. Easy terms."

The new party, which succeeded in unifying most socialists in the United States, focused on "immediate demands" (i.e., short-term concessions) and pledged to support the powerful American Federation of Labor. At various congresses, Malkiel advocated immediate reforms and support of the AFL and refused to wait passively for the socialist millennium. Like many socialists and female Jewish immigrant workers, she did not stand up to the AFL's xenophobia or its rejection of craft unionism—at least not publicly.[138]

More than as a rank-and-file party member, Malkiel should be remembered as a leading female activist and a tireless champion of women's progress. Her involvement with the Socialist Party of America spanned a lifetime of battles and remarkable changes. But long before the creation of the party, she had joined the Social Democratic Women's Federation, an influential association of German-American socialist women, created in 1897. Close to Clara Zetkin and the Second International, the association defended Socialist party fidelity at all costs and refused all cooperation with "bourgeois" feminists.

In her major study of women and American socialism, Mari Jo Buhle recounts the hesitations, passivity, and inconsistencies of the Socialist party—leaders as well as rank and file—regarding women's issues and the difficulties socialist partisans of women's emancipation encountered. At the founding meeting of the party in 1901, only 8 of the 128 delegates were women, and although the party endorsed "equal civil and political rights for men and women," the issue remained largely unaddressed until 1908. This is not surprising given the history of European socialism and of other parties in the United States.[139]

From the earliest days of the party, the issue of female emancipation had been entangled in a dispute over organizational autonomy versus centralization. Socialist women tended to orga-

---

138. Miller, "From Sweatshop Worker to Labor Leader," 196.
139. Buhle, *Women and American Socialism*, 105.

nize separately or to join the party depending on the setting. In the Midwest and Far West, for example, socialist women, inspired by the temperance movement and Christian socialism and a belief in women's culture, set up women's clubs that operated largely as educational societies.

Meanwhile, socialist women in industrial urban centers with large ethnic populations organized within the party structure. During the first six or seven years of the party's existence, the women, most of whom were activists' wives, worked in auxiliaries and ladies' branches of the party and left the leadership to the men. Reaching out from their female spheres, the Pillars of the Home, for example, organized charity sales, bazaars, choirs, and other fund-raising and membership events. Socialist leaders encouraged this "female mission." Occasionally, the men condescended to organize a "ladies' night" or "low-level" political exposés for them. A party cadre commented on the Women's Club in Haverhill, Massachusetts: "Doubtless these ladies discuss hats and shirtwaists at their meetings, sometimes. That is said to be woman's nature. But they do their work, anyhow and do it well."[140]

The years 1907–8 saw a massive influx of radical women, native-born and immigrant, into the urban sector of the party, which marked a significant change in its gender politics. Russian-Jewish women, Theresa Malkiel among them, played a major part in this shift. Reacting to the male-centered culture and influenced by Bund-type radical activism, these Jewish militants turned away from Socialist party bazaars and good works and demanded full political participation. One way to achieve this was by moving the women from auxiliaries into party locals.

Back in 1904–5, some Socialist party women had grumbled about their husbands' disregard for their wives' political inter-

---

140. Ibid., 122–24.

ests. They had luxuriated, nevertheless, in separatist sisterhood.[141] Now, as members of the ranks, they confronted the full
brunt of their male comrades' sexist attitudes. Some women deplored party members' old-fashioned views on the family,
which, at best, confined women to the role of their husbands',
brothers', or fathers' supporters. Others struggled with crass
misogyny based on the crudest biological thinking. At one
point, for example, Malkiel ridiculed a comrade who extolled
sexual prejudice. By placing women in the category of animals,
he condescended to endow them with instinctive and intuitive
qualities superior to those of men.[142]

Many party members, male and female, acknowledged the
existence of the discrimination. Exasperated by the party's
scornful attitude, women clamored to achieve equal and recognized participation. One dramatic gesture in this direction was
the creation in 1907 by Josephine Conger Kaneko of the magazine *Socialist Woman,* later renamed the *Progressive Woman.*

Through the early years of the century, demands for the wom-
en's vote heightened tensions within the party. By 1907–8,
female militants were caught in an uncomfortable dilemma.
On the one hand, the mainstream suffrage movement had ex-
panded: many New York City groups had merged into the
Woman Suffrage party.[143] On the other hand, in 1907, the Second International encouraged socialists to agitate for women's
suffrage but unequivocally forbade them from forming alliances
with "bourgeois" women and organizations. In this class-versus-
gender dilemma, Theresa Malkiel, a self-styled "Socialist and
suffragette," preserved both her socialist integrity and her free-

---

141. One wife related, "In the six years in which my husband has been a
socialist, he has a good deal of time been interested in the local and in public
meetings; and he has never asked me to attend any of them with him" (Buhle,
"Women and the Socialist Party," 40).

142. Malkiel, "Where Do We Stand on the Woman Question?" 161.

143. Tax, *Rising of the Women,* 170.

dom of action.[144] "I am a Socialist first, then a woman," she declared.[145] She regarded the vote for women as an obstacle to the progress of socialism and proclaimed her priorities to be the class struggle and deep social change beyond specific political reforms. Like many socialists, she warned of the dangers of collaboration with middle-class suffragists.

At the same time, Malkiel saw the vote as essential to women's emancipation and appreciated the special dynamism of women's struggles, insisting that "woman's true liberation will be brought about by herself." Should women fail to confront the contradictions of their predicament, they ran the risk of building "expectations on the future freedom and at the same time calmly submitting to the present oppression."[146] Malkiel urged socialists to act quickly in favor of suffrage, for she saw "the capitalists . . . on the verge of giving women the right to vote."[147] If they did not act quickly, weary of vacillations and fluctuations in the socialist camp about "cooperation" with suffragists, working women might turn away from the party toward bourgeois organizations.

The creation of the Woman's National Committee (WNC) in 1908 marked a turning point in the party's recognition of women's issues and in its views on separatism versus integration. A subcommittee of five was formed to foster educational work among women and children, to write propaganda, and to investigate labor conditions. This coordination and expansion of women's activities under the aegis of the party tended to shrink the independent sector of the socialist women's movement and to result in a shift in power away from the partisans of

---

144. Malkiel, "Theresa Malkiel," 2.

145. Socialist Party, *Proceedings*, 185.

146. Malkiel, "Where Do We Stand?" 161.

147. Malkiel, "Some Impressions on the New York Socialist Women's Conference."

women's autonomy in auxiliaries and clubs toward the defenders of centralization.

Theresa Malkiel was elected to the WNC in 1909 and was reelected three times in the seven years of the committee's existence. A delegate to three out of its four subsequent congresses, she was in charge of contacts with women socialists in Europe.[148] A full-fledged party functionary, she was also appointed to several executive positions.[149]

The party's move toward integrating women's issues was bound to please Theresa Malkiel, who had never been a separatist. One cause, however, drove her to organize independently: the plight of immigrant women workers, which throughout her life remained the issue closest to her heart.

Despite her middle-class status, Malkiel always identified herself as a Jewish immigrant and a sweatshop worker. Dissatisfied with the party's efforts in this area, in 1907 she organized a local group, the Women's Progressive Society of Yonkers, while maintaining her party membership. Reflecting the ethnic diversity of New York and dominated by foreign-speaking women, the group soon became Branch 1 of the autonomous Socialist Women's Society of New York.

Prejudice against immigrant women, Malkiel thought, affected both the higher and lower echelons of the Socialist party. At the leadership level, Jewish immigrants were not adequately represented, although two of the other four seats on the WNC during her first term were held by immigrant women.[150] The situation had more serious consequences, however, and Malkiel strived to make immigrant women workers a special concern of the party. She encouraged party members to go to tenements,

<hr />

148. A meeting was to take place in Vienna in August 1914 at the same time as the Congress for the Second International.

149. Miller, "From Sweatshop Worker to Labor Leader," 195.

150. Ibid., 199.

to establish contacts with foreign-language socialist federations, and to help immigrants translate propaganda pamphlets into their own languages. Each ethnic group elected a delegate to a WNC commission in charge of propaganda among women who did not speak English, and soon delegates representing South Slav, Jewish, Finnish, and German women joined her organization. Questionnaires assessed their socioeconomic profile and investigated their views on religion, unions, and women's vote. This information was distributed to all the foreign-language groups. [151]

Theresa Malkiel's lifelong concern for immigrant working women reflected both her personal and political experiences. As a former "working girl," the issue had the immediacy and simplicity of daily life. In its early years, however, the Socialist party still harbored prejudices against women in the workplace, inherited from the German-American reverence for the class-conscious hausfrau and Ferdinand Lassalle's desire to restrict women to a domestic role. [152] As socialists came to recognize the permanence of waged labor under capitalism, their theories failed to take into account the specific features of women's work, such as the contribution of household labor to the economy.

Malkiel thought and wrote much on the subject, notably in *Woman and Freedom, To a Working Woman,* and *To a Union Man's Wife.* [153] These and other pamphlets she wrote, many of them undated, were published by the Co-operative Press. Like other radical women in the party, she was convinced that women's work would remain a fact of life. She argued that the only weapon against severe exploitation in the workplace was the

151. Ibid., 200.

152. Buhle, *Women and American Socialism,* 179.

153. Malkiel, *Woman and Freedom,* Microfilm no. 5420, *To a Working Woman,* Microfilm no. 5417, *To a Union Man's Wife,* Microfilm no. 5416, Tamiment Library, New York University.

"two-arm" strategy: organizing in unions and becoming socialist. Only a victorious class struggle could end women's oppression, she said, and she urged women to join those "in whom the sacred fire burns . . . those who will make the trumpet sound announcing the advent of liberty."[154] In an article in the *New York Call* of December 4, 1909, she rejoiced that all the women strikers had had their consciousnesses raised and joined the union. Writing in the flowery and prophetic rhetoric of the day, she proclaimed: "They have suddenly caught a glimpse of a new fairyland and are stretching hurriedly their long idle wings, raising their bowed heads preparatory to taking flight into it."

Confined by the boundaries of her socialist allegiance, Malkiel did not always perceive the interaction of sex and class on women's predicament. She did, however, here and there in her writings identify the "double burden" as it specifically related to women's gendered situation and oppression at home and at work. "They want your muscles," she said to the working woman. "You are not paid for your housework," she said to the worker's wife. She urged women to relinquish romantic expectations of marriage and to expect only grueling, interminable, unpaid labor.[155] It is not clear whether Malkiel saw the economic value in domestic labor as some of her co-workers did and demanded that it be recognized.[156] Unlike some party members, she does not appear to have considered household work an anomaly or an injustice or to have thought it should be remunerated or abolished.[157]

After the first decade of the twentieth century, the question of women's industrial work hit the headlines. "The women's

---

154. Malkiel, "To the Working Woman."
155. Malkiel, "My Sisters in Toil."
156. Robinson, "Work and Housework."
157. See Lanfersieck, "How Shall Mothers Be Recompensed under Socialism?" and Walden, "Women's Slavery."

strikes" of 1909–11 in New York and Chicago turned women's labor and unionization into mass concerns.[158] Following the "two-arm" strategy, socialist women proselytized in the rapidly expanding women's sector of the garment industry in New York and other large cities in the East. They recruited women into the Socialist party and persuaded them to join labor unions. The birth of two totally different organizations—the International Ladies' Garment Workers' Union (a "new union") in 1900 and the Women's Trade Union League in 1903—helped socialist activists get a footing in the shirtwaist trade.

When the shirtwaist strike erupted in November 1909, Malkiel, a member of the WTUL's local executive board and one of a twelve-member strike committee elected by the WNC, plunged into the fray. The *New York Call,* on November 27, 1909, mentioned her appeal to all volunteer speakers; on December 3, her speech at the Liptzkin Theatre before the march to City Hall; and, on January 13, 1910, a public protest to the police for their obscene behavior toward a young striker.

But it was her journalistic work, mostly in the *New York Call,* that made her presence felt inside and outside the party. Few weeks went by without an article by Malkiel. And in 1910, she even wrote a long pamphlet to celebrate the Uprising of the 20,000.

The question of the vote remained a major concern for Malkiel throughout her life. It lurked behind the scenes of the shirtwaist strike, in which women fought heroic battles on the labor front and joined unions under the Socialist party banner while remaining deprived of the franchise. Socialist women regarded the vote as a basic political right, but they were not in a position to make it a priority. In contrast, labor militants immersed themselves in the struggle and kept aloof from the issue of the vote, which they regarded as largely the prerogative of the

---

158. Buhle, *Women and American Socialism,* 190.

"fine ladies" and unrelated to working women's problems. Like other Socialist party women, Malkiel had to steer a frustrating course between the party's reluctance to espouse the vote for women, its dogmatic injunctions, and her own commitment to women's emancipation.

Malkiel's pragmatism occasionally led her to cooperate with bourgeois organizations, such as the National Woman's Suffrage Association, and, after the 1910 party congress, she threw herself into the party's battle for suffragism. Following the directives of the International, she founded several suffrage clubs on the Lower East Side and in Harlem, the Bronx, and Queens that featured a mix of political discussions and cultural activities. She directed the New York City campaign for the vote on a referendum bill sponsored by the state legislature in 1913, and she organized committees, called meetings, and wrote pamphlets and a women's column in the *Jewish Daily Forward.*

After the defeat of the referendum, however, the central party committee decided to retrench on women's affairs. It withdrew delegates and funds from the suffrage campaign committee and stopped supporting the *Progressive Woman.* Some militants withdrew from the Woman's National Committee, which disappeared, along with the *Progressive Woman,* in 1914. Undaunted, Malkiel protested these decisions and claimed to have increased party membership in the city by 25 percent during the suffrage campaign.[159] In the pamphlet *More Serious than Funny,* she bitterly denounced the party's hostility to the WNC.[160] She vainly argued that in disbanding the committee, the party had ignored half the proletariat and abandoned women to the conservative influences of the churches. In 1915, another referendum confirmed the leadership's decision. In spite of the obstacles, Malkiel tried to maintain a women's network and to revive the

159. Ibid., 233–35.

160. Tax, *Rising of the Women,* 195; the pamphlet was in the *American Socialist,* April 24, 1915.

suffrage campaign in 1917. But without the party's support, such efforts were doomed to failure. Despite her disappointment, Malkiel stayed in the party and fought against World War I and for women's suffrage.

In addition to political issues, Theresa Malkiel expressed her views on sexuality, family, and gender roles. To her, the present was marked by oppression, exploitation, even degradation, but there was a rosy socialist future of equality, happiness, and fulfillment. She denounced and analyzed women's "double burden" as industrial and domestic workers and their dependence on men. "Woman is the slave of a slave to day," she wrote. Convinced that women should escape from their domestic jail, she demystified both conventional gender roles and the glorification of the home.[161] Like Engels, she argued that when a woman worked all day in mills and factories, "there is no home to destroy."[162] Those who accused socialists of smashing the home perpetrated blatant mystification, she said, and used the myth of home and homemaker to reinforce women's domestic bondage and discredit socialism.

Yet when Malkiel pictured women and the family in the society of the future, her outlook was informed by the traditional ethics of social purity that prevailed in bourgeois society and the Socialist party until 1910. The agitation of the "new intellectuals" who favored sexual liberation, sensual fulfillment, and birth control and were against the prison of family ties seems to have passed her by.[163] What she saw as "the depravity of sexual life" could only victimize women[164]; there was a rigid diadic pattern of man's lust and woman's purity, male power and woman's helplessness: "the unchecked passions of husbands

---

161. Malkiel, "Socialism."
162. Malkiel, "Capitalism and the Home," 4.
163. Buhle, *Women and American Socialism*, 249, 257 *passim*.
164. Malkiel, "The Vampire."

preying upon hapless and helpless wives." The Manichaean Christian discourse of nineteenth-century advocates of women's rights clouded her socialist vision. Although Malkiel saw the "free woman" under socialism achieving equality in society and within marriage, emotionally she still adhered to the Victorian stereotype of pure womanhood. The "feminine instinct," she wrote, would lead women to "save the souls of the children as well as their bodies and thus raise the ideal men and women of the future." Beyond this magical influence, she would be "a capable mother, a cheerful companion and helpmate."[165] Not for her the lures of "free love" or communal living. Malkiel believed that under socialism women would be better wives and mothers. Her short autobiographical piece in the *Progressive Woman* presents her as the paradigm of the perfect wife and perfect militant. Emotionally charged clichés such as "model housekeeper," "household duties," and "good wife and mother," combined with the piece's didactic goal, convey her belief in the superiority of the image of wife and mother.[166]

After 1920, Theresa Malkiel cut back on her activities in the Socialist party. True to her former goals, however, she spent her later years promoting adult education for immigrant women and helping them become naturalized. Her obituary in the *New York Times* (November 18, 1949) mentions her involvement in the Brooklyn Adult Student Association, where poor immigrant women could enjoy classes and attend a summer camp.[167] We know too little about Malkiel's private life and personal responses to integrate the public and the private in her life. Besides, womanly modesty about private matters, combined with her absorbing life, probably kept her from making personal testimonies.

---

165. Malkiel, "The Free Woman," 7.
166. Malkiel, "Theresa Malkiel," 2.
167. Miller, "From Sweatshop Worker to Labor Leader," 204.

Malkiel's goals and interests did not vary over time. Rather, they alternated in response to changes in the Socialist party and political events. Like a good socialist, she believed in the class struggle and the fight for social justice. But she also seemed convinced of the imperative need to defend women's issues. In the two areas in which she was most active, women's suffrage and the cause of immigrant women, she probably felt betrayed or abandoned by the Socialist party. For if it is true that the suffrage campaign was successful among socialists, then the party must have lost interest and buried the issue during World War I. Nor were the support and defense of immigrant women, to which Malkiel devoted much of her life, among the party's major interests.

Malkiel's Diary: *History, Fiction, Propaganda*

I n the last ten years, the Uprising of the 20,000 has gained an important place in the historical record. Theresa Malkiel's *Diary of a Shirtwaist Striker,* however, has been consigned to oblivion since its publication in 1910, dismissed or at best regarded as "a piece of socialist propaganda."

In recent years, historians and literary critics, who challenge the canons of "good writing," have become more attentive to popular works that both reflect and were shaped by contemporary values. An epic of female working-class life, Malkiel's book comments on socialist politics and culture in the early twentieth century while creating fictional characters, plot, and suspense.

The Diary of a Shirtwaist Striker was published by the Cooperative Press, which specialized in socialist literature, a few months after the end of the shirtwaist strike. Excerpts had appeared in serial form in the *New York Call* from April 15 to May 14, 1910, under the title "From the Diary of a Striking Waist Maker." The number of copies that were printed and the details of distribution are unknown. What we do know is that the clothbound edition cost fifty cents and the paperback twenty-five cents and that the book was advertised in socialist circles and in one issue of the *Progressive Woman* (November 10, 1910). Promising the audience a heroic story of working-class life, the insert urged, "DON'T FAIL TO READ THIS BOOK. GIVE IT A BIG CIRCULATION. IT SHOWS WHAT WOMEN CAN AND ARE DOING, IN THE INDUSTRIAL WORLD."

"To the nameless heroines of the Shirtwaist Makers' Strike, this Diary is lovingly dedicated by the author." Reminiscent of a dedication to war heroes, this inscription on the opening page told Malkiel's readers of her love and admiration for her characters. Malkiel's motivations for writing a hymn of praise to needleworkers stem from her adolescent years when she herself was a Jewish immigrant from Eastern Europe, an exploited sweatshop worker, a union organizer, and a socialist militant. When the strike began, she had been out of the sweatshop for nine years, the wife of a prosperous lawyer since 1900, and the mother of a little girl. But she would never forget her deep commitment to socialist politics and to immigrant women.

Malkiel's decision to write an account of the strike in the form of a fictional diary served several purposes. Whatever the book's literary merits or demerits, the diary form enabled Malkiel to combine in an effective way her concerns about social issues and her literary skills. As a reporter and militant, Malkiel had a vested interest in presenting events accurately and in the correct time sequence. A cross between John Reed's *Ten Days That Shook the World* and Emile Zola's *Germinal*, the *Diary* provides a chronology of key events. Some pertain directly to the struggle (workshops, picketing, and arrests), some to public relations (meetings and demonstrations, the "mink brigade" party for the "girls," and the Socialist party reception for the strikers released from prison). Others relate to political and strategic issues. Malkiel was a conscientious historian: we can reconstruct the events of the strike and identify characters from the diary entries. Furthermore, the form helps readers keep the complex facts straight and heightens the dramatic tension.

In addition to providing a convenient structure for organizing a packed sequence of events, the diary form proves to be a useful device for presenting the heroine's changing consciousness. Day by day, over a three-month period, Mary undergoes a process of moral and political apprenticeship, reappraisal, and change. By linking the world inside and outside without totally merging them, the diary form enables Malkiel to demonstrate her heroine's openness to both emotional and political evolution.

The diary form also freed Malkiel from the constraints of a conventional plot. Diary writing provides its own story line and a structure that eliminates the need for contrived transitions. Events seem to flow easily from one day to the next in a smooth sequence. Thus Malkiel could indulge her heroine's spontaneity by starting an entry with exclamations or an incomplete sentence, by addressing an imaginary reader, or by using flashbacks.

The choice of the first person legitimizes the book's subjectivity. It enables Malkiel to present her own point of view while distancing herself from the subject, thereby lightening the burden of historical accuracy and objectivity. The first-person narrative creates intimacy between writer and reader, but it also gives the author leeway vis-à-vis her characters. Writing with the voice of one of the "girls" deepens identification between the heroine and the strikers and sympathizers. At the same time, the reader can identify with the heroine and share her vision, pain, and progress. Malkiel may have also thought that the informal style of the first person would make the book accessible to working-class readers.

Solidarity with her co-workers and a desire to retrieve her past were powerful motives for Malkiel in writing the *Diary*. But as a socialist activist, she also had urgent political motives. The strike was rocking the labor world, redefining relationships between ethnic groups, unions, and management and between women of lower and upper classes. Malkiel wanted to tell the story within a socialist framework so as to win more workers to socialism. Her concern was more than justified in that other pressure groups were wooing the strikers and trying to appropriate the strike.

So as to tell the story and convey the message, Malkiel chose as her heroine and narrator not a recent Russian or Italian immigrant, as one would expect, but "a free-born American" whose father was an American and a union member and whose mother was a housewife most of the time. For someone as rooted in her immigrant identity as Malkiel, this choice deserves investigation. Creating a heroine who was better integrated and better paid than she was highlighted significant aspects of the labor scene, the immigrants' oppression, and the widespread xenophobia. As the story opens, Mary discovers the hostility encountered by foreign workers. Even in her own home, her father and fiancé look down on the "East Side girls." Malkiel apparently sensed the effectiveness of using a native-born apolitical worker rather than a politically educated immigrant to stress the place of the ghetto in American society.

Choosing an American-born woman as her heroine enables Malkiel to sing hymns of praise to the "noble Jew girls" and to take the reader through a process of discovery and exploration. Mary, the nonimmigrant, and Malkiel, the insider, could freely eulogize the strikers' courage, heroism, and intelligence. This combination of identification and distance serves to show readers that Mary did not join their battle instinctively but of her own free will. These twists and turns of the story are effective tools of antiracist pedagogy.

Making her heroine an American also helped Malkiel, the socialist propagandist, make an important strategic point. American-born workers had a bad reputation in the needle trades as prejudiced against Jewish and Italian workers. They did not perceive themselves as exploited and often refused to strike; employers thus found them an ideal hunting ground for scabs. One of the major goals of the Socialist party and of the Women's Trade Union League was to recruit American workers. Through Mary's story of enlightenment, Malkiel was telling labor organizers not to give up on slow-moving, native-born Americans. In time, socialist propaganda would affect all sectors of labor and turn reconciliation between ethnic groups into a reality.

Another possible reason for Malkiel's choice of an American heroine might have been her fear of anti-Semitic reactions from middle-class WASP readers.

In the bildungsroman tradition, *The Diary of a Shirtwaist Striker* tells a story of experience and change. Typically the youthful heroes (rarely heroines) of these novels of apprenticeship travel from one point to the next in time, space, and consciousness. During this process, socialization interacts with interiority, the collective with the individual dimension. Here, in the short time span of the strike, the heroine grows from youth to mature adult, from innocence to experience, from carefree superficiality to enlightened happiness. This story of progress unfolds in the framework of twentieth-century socialism.

Mary is first presented as an ordinary young woman who is interested in earning higher wages and in her impending marriage. Better paid than most other "girls," she proudly belongs to a family in which neither her wage-earning mother nor grandmother belongs to a union. Initially, Mary does not take the walkout seriously. Later, intrigued by the strikers' self-sacrifice and enthusiasm, she learns about the wretched lives of the immigrant women workers—their low wages and the squalor of their tenements—and comes to admire their endurance and fearless energy.

Almost at once, too quickly perhaps in the context of the story, Mary supports the strike. As she grows closer to the Jewish and Italian women, she becomes aware of her own privileged status but also that all is not well, even for American "girls."

Whatever one's origin, a worker is nothing but a "hand." From here on, with disconcerting rapidity, Mary begins to see the world as divided into the exploited and the exploiters. Women stand virtually alone against the mammoth alliance of bosses, police, and the law. Mother Jones's inflammatory rhetoric confirms Mary's new sense of the "terrible war raging just now" or what Mary calls "the war for a bit of bread." In this uncertain battle, only struggle can give the young women self-respect; only organizing can give them power.

Echoing socialist values, Mary describes and analyzes the development of the strike, the organization of the bosses, and the hardships of the picket line, police brutality, and mass arrest. To the class struggle, Malkiel adds a dash of feminism consistent with her pamphlets. Mary supports union organization for women and all ethnic groups, as well as union recognition by employers. But unlike Malkiel, Mary berates the WTUL for its allegiance to the AFL, which was lukewarm about organizing women and unskilled labor. To the last, Mary fights for closed shops, the one major demand the strikers failed to win.

Mary's views of strike supporters, Socialist party women, and autonomous suffragists reflected those of Malkiel, the Socialist party, and the strikers. She feels only dislike and anger toward the "mink brigade" (the millionaire suffragists, like Alva Belmont and Anne Morgan), wallowing in their wealth. As to their agitation for women's suffrage, Mary's priorities echo Malkiel's: she insists that class equality is a more urgent goal than gender equality: "Us girls have something else to think of just now. We must see to it that we win the strike for bread and then we can start one for the ballot."

Malkiel belonged to the WTUL and has her heroine approve of its aims. Mary thus thinks highly of the political and human involvement of the league women and is touched that this "fine lot of women," most of whom were educated and well-off, participated in the strike out of a sense of social justice. She does not mention the embarrassing occasions that manifested differences of class and ethnic background. In Mary's edifying story of good versus evil, the "allies" belong unequivocally on the side of good.

Mary tells a tale of class awareness. But her struggle also teaches her about gender. In this respect, Mary's evolution differs somewhat from Malkiel's. Mary's discovery of exploitation at work and her subsequent experience of solidarity and resistance make her aware of the oppression in her private life. The tyranny of her family, particularly of her father, and of her fiancé echoes the tyranny at the workplace. No doubt, Malkiel had in mind party comrades, as well as countless workers, who in spite of their political progress still had their sexist attitudes intact. "Union is all good and well by itself, but it was never meant for the women," declares Mary's father.

From the outset, Mary has an instinctive sense of gender inequality that leads her to deconstruct conventional images. Inequality in the world of labor emerges as a much stronger theme than in Malkiel's pamphlets. Mary believes, for instance, that living conditions construct comparable gender identities. "Where's the difference between man and woman when it comes to work?" she asks, in effect refuting biological difference. Echoing Sojourner Truth, Mary exclaims, "Ain't I of the same flesh and bone as a man? I, too, was carried under a mother's heart. . . . I walk under the same sky and tread the same earth as men do."

Mary is quick to rebel against the double standard implicit in the attitudes of socialist comrades who find it unladylike for women to fight back and do not object to their being overworked and underpaid. Mary's denunciation of discrimination against women is dramatically highlighted in her changing perception of Jim. Her awareness of herself as a "soldier" in an army, a tree "in a great shady forest," grows into a sense of personal and collective identity. As a result of this change, she realizes that the power of her father and prospective husband is as arbitrary and crushing as her employer's.

Rejection of patriarchy develops out of the revolt against capitalism.

As Mary's new sense of self expands, she discovers that kinship with comrades, built on suffering and joy in struggle, is more powerful than blood ties. She distances herself from her parents and betrothed.

As she grows toward maturity, Mary recognizes more and more that her fiancé, like a prospective factory owner, feels threatened by her revolt against employers and the patriarchal family. Her independence challenges his male status. As the plot develops, Malkiel links class and gender oppression more forcefully than she ever did in her pamphlets.

The storyteller had to keep within the conventions of an edifying story yet needed a happy ending. Mary therefore had to be saved from spinsterhood, an all-too-common condition of women activists, militants of the Socialist party, and members of the WTUL, such as Pauline Newman, Rose Schneiderman, and Clara Lemlich. At the same time, in the context of the heroine's progress, Mary could not be forced into sexist oppression under the yoke of an average socialist husband. The only way out of the dilemma was a providential solution: Mary has to raise Jim to her own lofty heights.

This image of woman as guide and inspirer was part of the socialist gospel. Theresa Malkiel, who had presented herself as a perfect wife, mother, and militant in the *Progressive Woman*, incorporates those values into the *Diary*'s happy ending.[168] "Having entered the path of truth," Mary converts the man she loves to socialism. The narrative spells out the steps of Jim's conversion, how his head and heart open to suffering and injustice. Awakened to this vision by Mary's quasi-magical influence, Jim can overcome his limitations and recognize her autonomy. How he suddenly links class and gender oppression remains unex-

---

168. Malkiel, "Theresa Malkiel," 2.

plained, but once he has "seen the light," he has no qualms about giving the union the money he had saved for Mary's Christmas present. Mary now embodies the oppressed, the Cause.

Malkiel's belief in women's moral superiority was part of a world view that combined both Christian and Jewish values. She makes Mary the priestess of the socialist millennium: "She will unfurl her standard to the air . . . and will establish a system of brotherhood. As man's companion she will produce the world's wealth for use and not for profit, for the benefit of all without distinction of race, creed and sex."[169]

The Victorian Angel in the house and the priestess of the socialist millennium are strange bedfellows, but bedfellows nevertheless. Except for asserting the equality of men and women and railing against patriarchal authority, Mary hardly questions the conventional role of wife, mother, and homemaker. She occasionally objects to the validity of marriage for a working woman, but she stops short of criticizing the prevailing family pattern. "If I ever got married, I'd want to mind our home and take care of our children," Mary says. Theresa Malkiel went further. To the model of the Victorian female, Mary contributed a new feature, militancy. Malkiel, too, had optimistically claimed to be the perfect wife and mother and militant.[170]

The socialist woman internalizes the claim to perfection but substitutes a political mission for Christian calling. This is close to the outlook of the "social housekeepers," programmed to radiate their benevolent influence from the home to the world outside. The party could only approve. This view contradicted a common observation, however, that marriage put an end to political involvement for Jewish female workers.[171]

As for Jim, Malkiel makes sure that he becomes a worthwhile companion. Although handicapped by his male privileges, and

---

169. Malkiel, *Woman and Freedom*.
170. Malkiel, "Theresa Malkiel," 2.
171. Waldinger, "Another Look at the ILGWU," 91.

therefore slowed down in his progress toward the light, Mary puts him on the right road and from then on finds many reasons to admire him.

The ending of the *Diary* integrates Malkiel's moderate feminism with socialist visions of the future. Though understated, Mary's happiness points to the socialist dream: man and woman, like two halves of a whole person, walking hand in hand toward a better world, in a mood of utopian cheerfulness. A repertoire of socialist and union songs illustrated these themes: "It's Better with a Union Man," "A Little Girl Comrade," and others. [172] Their naive lyrics with their overblown metaphors celebrated the ideal socialist couple. [173] In one, the girl longs to be the Virginia creeper around the vigorous oak. But the oak is unavailable:

So I'll lift my head up high
And be a pretty tree so straight
Forever reaching towards the sky,
I'll brave the brave winds of fate.

Who knows! Perhaps when I am grown tall,
And am a lovely graceful tree
The sturdy oak beyond the wall
May reach his brawny arms to me,
And we'll shake hands, my comrade tree. [174]

Theresa Malkiel's tract provided a message of comfort and good cheer for female industrial fighters on the front line. Far from being confined to socialist theory or dogma, the stuff of her politics was experience and emotions. Mary's awakening to

---

172. The first song tells the story of Bertha, "a winsome and class conscious lass" courted by a nonunion man "with a leer." Fortunately, union love triumphs. Conclusion: "It's better with a union man; you'll never go wrong if you follow this plan: it's better with a a union man."

173. Alloy, *Working Women's Music*, 20.

174. Verse by Nannie Parker in *Progressive Woman*, February 1911, 12.

social injustice is a process of conversion and change of the heart rather than a political experience. Like early socialists, she linked the fight for justice with religious evangelical fervor, in "the millennial Protestant tradition common to Populist and temperance circles."[175] Reminiscent of William Blake, the book takes its theme of the corrupt city, the discovery of degradation and evil at every corner, from the same inspiration.

Both the *Diary's* exhortation to justice and its prophetic voice evoke the labor churches and the evangelical tradition. The spiritual message predicts the Second Coming and a socialist golden age. A scene in the *Diary* illustrates this inspiration. Mary hears a minister preach a Sunday sermon at the Church of Ascension. Switching from the New Testament to socialist rhetoric, he translates Matthew's promise, "The meek shall inherit the earth," into the "army of the unemployed."

Mary's conversion within this mixed gospel amounts to a new birth. Leaving father and mother, she embraces a whole army. As a newborn, empowered woman, she will awaken the new man in Jim. Women occupy a privileged place in this Christian socialist utopia, as they did in many revival groups. "And as through her cometh man's life, so through her shall come his liberation," the minister says. By the end of the book, we have come full circle: the socialist gospel has endorsed the Victorian female saviour, and the socialist activist has revolutionized the male/female relationship in marriage. Mary's ambition is perfect equality and sharing. Man and wife are "friend and companion," their duty, as Mary defines it, to "soothe and comfort, consult, and advise."

A didactic piece, designed to inspire workers to organize against capitalism, *The Diary of a Shirtwaist Striker* still speaks to us. Besides reading like a suspense story, it vividly and accu-

---

175. Buhle, *Women and American Socialism*, 116.

rately recreates the world of working-class Jewish labor and culture, family, and gender relations at the turn of the century. For all its old-fashioned overtones and clichés, Theresa Malkiel's story conveys a strong message that class and gender emancipation are inseparable.

Bibliography

Alloy, Evelyn, ed. *Working Women's Music: The Songs and Struggles of Women in the Cotton Mills, Textile Plants and Needle Trades.* Somerville, Mass.: New England Free Press, 1976.

Baxandall, Rosalyn, Linda Gordon, and Susan Reverby. *American Working Women.* New York: Vintage Books, 1976.

Buhle, Mari Jo. *Women and American Socialism, 1780–1920.* Urbana: University of Illinois Press, 1981.

———. "Women and the Socialist Party." *Radical America* 4 (1970).

Cameron, Ardis. "Bread and Roses Revisited: Women's Culture and Working-Class Activism in the Lawrence Strike of 1912." *See* Milkman.

Clark, Sue Ainslie, and Edith Wyatt. "Working-Girls' Budgets: The Shirtwaist-makers and Their Strike." *McClure's,* November 1910.

Dreier, Mary. *Margaret Dreier Robins: Her Life, Letters and Work.* New York: Island Press Cooperative, 1950.

Dubofsky. Melvyn. *When Workers Organize: New York City in the Progressive Era.* Amherst: University of Massachusetts Press, 1968.

Dye, Nancy Schrom. *As Equals and as Sisters: Feminism, the Labor Movement, and the Women's Trade Union League of New York.* Columbia: University of Missouri Press, 1980.

Ertel, Rachel. *Le roman juif américain: une écriture minoritaire.* Paris: Payot, 1980.

Ewen, Elizabeth. *Immigrant Women in the Land of Dollars: Life and Culture on the Lower East Side, 1890–1925.* New York: Monthly Review Press, 1985.

Flynn, Elizabeth Gurley. *The Rebel Girl: An Autobiography.* New York: International Publishers, 1955.

Goodman, Pearl, and Elsa Ueland. "The Shirtwaist Trade." *Journal of Political Economy,* December 1910.

Henry, Alice. *The Trade Union Woman.* New York: D. Appleton, 1915.

Hillquit, Morris. *Loose Leaves from a Busy Life.* New York: Macmillan, 1934.

Howe, Irving. *World of Our Fathers.* New York: Harcourt Brace Jovanovich, 1976.

Howe, Irving, and Eliezer Greenberg, eds. *Voices from the Yiddish.* New York: Schocken Books, 1975.

Hyman, Colette A. "Labor Organizing and Female Institution Building." *See* Milkman.

Jensen, Joan M. "The Great Uprisings, 1900–1920." *See* Jensen and Davidson.

Jensen, Joan M., and Sue Davidson, eds. *A Needle, a Bobbin, a Strike: Women Needleworkers in America.* Philadelphia: Temple University Press, 1984.

The Jewish People: Past and Present. New York: Jewish Encyclopedic Handbooks, 1955.

Kessler-Harris, Alice. "Organizing the Unorganizable: Three Jewish Women and Their Union." *Labor History,* Winter 1976.

———. *Out to Work: A History of Wage-Earning Women in the United States.* New York: Oxford University Press, 1982.

Kessner, Thomas. *The Golden Door: Italian and Jewish Immigrant Mobility in New York City, 1880–1915.* New York: Oxford University Press, 1977.

Lanfersieck, W. "How Shall Mothers Be Recompensed under Socialism?" *Progressive Woman,* March 1910.

Lemlich, Clara. "Why Waistmakers Strike." *New York Evening Journal,* November 26, 1909.

Levine, Louis. *The Women Garment Workers: A History of the International Ladies' Garment Workers' Union.* 1924. Reprint. New York: Arno Press, 1969.

Malkiel, Theresa. "Capitalism and the Home." *Socialist Woman,* January 1909.

———. "The Free Woman." *Socialist Woman,* October 1908.

———. "My Sisters in Toil." *Socialist Woman,* July 1900.

———. "Socialism." *Progressive Woman,* May 1910.

———. "Some Impressions on the New York Socialist Women's Conference." *Socialist Woman,* August 1908.

———. "Theresa Malkiel." *Progressive Woman,* May 1909.

———. "To the Working Woman." *Socialist Woman,* July 1908.

———. "The Vampire." *Progressive Woman,* April 1910.

———. "Where Do We Stand on the Woman Question?" *International Socialist Review,* August 1909.

———. "Woman and the Socialist Party." *Socialist Woman,* May 1908.

Marot, Helen. *American Labor Unions.* 1914. Reprint. New York: Arno Press, 1969.

75

————. "A Woman's Strike." *See* Tax.

————. "A Woman's Strike: An Appreciation of the Shirtwaist Makers of New York." *See* Baxandall, Gordon, and Reverby.

Menes, Abraham. "The East Side and the Jewish Labor Movement." *See* Howe and Greenberg.

Miller, Sally M. "From Sweatshop Worker to Labor Leader: Theresa Malkiel, a Case Study." *American Jewish History,* December 1978.

Milkman, Ruth, ed. *Women, Work, and Protest: A Century of United States Women's Labor History.* New York: Routledge & Kegan Paul, 1985.

Neidle, Cecyle S. *America's Immigrant Women.* New York: Hippocrene Books, 1976.

Pidgeon, Mary Elizabeth. *Toward Better Working Conditions for Women: Methods and Policies of the National Women's Trade Union League of America.* Bulletin no. 252. Washington, D.C.: Department of Labor, Women's Bureau, 1953.

Rischin, Moses. *The Promised City: New York's Jews, 1870–1914.* Cambridge, Mass.: Harvard University Press, 1962.

Robinson, Lilian. "Daughters of the Shtetl." *Women's Review of Books,* September 1988.

Robinson, L. P. "Work and Housework." *Socialist Woman,* August 1908.

Schneiderman, Rose, with Lucy Goldthwaite. *All for One.* New York: Paul S. Eriksson, 1967.

————. "Triangle Memorial Speech." *See* Wertheimer.

Schofield, Ann. "The Uprising of the 20,000." *See* Jensen and Davidson.

Scott, Joan Wallach, and Owen Hufton. "Women in History." *Past and Present,* November 1983.

Seidman, Joel. *The Needle Trades.* New York: Farrar and Rhinehart, 1942.

Socialist Party of America. *Proceedings of National Congress, 1910.* Chicago: Socialist Party of America, 1910.

The Souvenir History of the Strike. New York: Ladies' Waist and Dressmakers' Union, 1910.

Tax, Meredith. *The Rising of the Women: Feminist Solidarity and Class Conflict, 1880–1917.* New York: Monthly Review Press, 1980.

Wald, Lillian. *The House on Henry Street.* New York: Dover Publications, 1971.

Walden, May. "Woman's Slavery." *Socialist Woman,* May 1907.

Waldinger, Roger. "Another Look at the International Ladies' Garment Workers' Union: Women, Industry Structure and Collective Action." *See* Milkman.

Wertheimer, Barbara Mayer. *We Were There: The Story of Working Women in America.* New York: Pantheon Books, 1977.

Yezierska, Anzia. *Bread Givers.* 1925. Reprint. New York: G. Braziller, 1975.

The Diary of a
Shirtwaist Striker

Theresa Serber Malkiel

*To the nameless heroines of the Shirtwaist Makers' Strike
this Diary is lovingly dedicated by the author. . . .*

November 23, 1909

Ha, ha, ha! that's a joke. By Jove, it is. I'm a striker. I wonder what Jim'll have to say to this?

I must say I really don't know why I became one—I went down just because everybody else in the workroom did. They did try to explain it all to us girls, but all I could make out from the woman's speech was when she raised her eyes to the ceiling and exclaimed, like they do on the stage: "Sisters, mine, we are all with you!"—the lot of good it'll do us.

Oh, pshaw, if one was to believe all they tell you down there! The idea of their telling us that us girls are nothin' but slaves. Perhaps they are, but not I. I'm a free-born American, I am.

Some of them speakers look too silly for anything, especially that one with the long bushy hair. An' the way he screamed at the top of his voice, one would think that the house is on fire. I wonder if it hurts him—this strike does?

I guess Jim wouldn't mind my being a striker if he knew what fun I'm getting out of it. But I know better, he's that strict about all such things. I can just hear him call me an anarchist. And yet, it's a good thing, this strike is; it makes you feel like a real grown-up person. But I wish I'd feel about it like them Jew girls do. Why, their eyes flash fire as soon as they commence to talk about the strike—and the lot of talk they can put up—at times they make a body feel like two cents.

I simply can't get over the way little Ray Goldovsky jumped on a chair and suddenly, without a minute's notice, stopped the electricity. I must say, it's nothing but her bravery that took us all. Why, we were simply stunned. And Mr. Hayman, too, was taken off his feet. Before you could say Jack Robinson we all rose, slipped on our duds and marched down the stairs, shouting, yelling and giggling about our walkout, as they called it.

From there we went down in a body to Clinton Hall, an' Lord! I never saw so many people at once in my life, as I did there this afternoon. Talk about pushing and shoving, I don't see how some of us weren't killed in that crowd. I think they're the funniest people out; I almost split my sides laughing at some of them. And the way they were jabbering with each other, an' quarreling about that strike, you'd really think their whole life depended on it.

I ain't a bit sorry that I did go down. What do I lose by it? Mr. Hayman will be only too glad to take me back. Meanwhile I'm having stacks of fun. Ma don't know that I ain't working. What was the use of telling her? I suppose the whole thing will be over in a day or two, and what she don't know don't hurt her.

I hope it won't last long! Oh! well, I won't be in it if it does. It's all good and well as a novelty, but who cares to get excited over it and take it to heart, the way Sarah, for instance, does. No, thanks, none of that for mine.

I'm surprised that Mr. Hayman didn't show up this afternoon; they were all so sure that he'd settle within a few hours. I guess it has been the girls' own imagination. It makes me smile when I think of being labeled; but what was I to do? Everybody gave in their name, so I had to give mine and a dime with it. They warned me that I can't get my union book unless I pay in the rest, $1.15 in all. As if a body cares for their old book. What in the world do I want with a union? My mother and grandmother have gone through life without belonging to one and I guess I, too, can get along without it.

The only thing that keeps me with them is that it may help those poor devils who have to work for three and four dollars a week. It's but very few of the girls that make such wages as I do. And I believe they must have a real hard time of it. They look it. It was enough to break one's heart to see some of them. Perhaps it will be over tomorrow.

November 24

Well, well, I think this strike is a more serious business than I thought, otherwise the papers wouldn't make so much of it. Why, every one of them is full of the strike and strikers; we are made so much of. It really feels good to be somebody. It even gave me courage to tell ma that I, too, am a striker. Of course I had to give her a whopper—had to tell her that Mr. Hayman closed up shop when the girls went out. He's just the one to do it. He's sure to keep it up, if only for spite. I wonder why he hates the union so much?

It's strange, when you come to think of all the noise us girls have made for the last two days. Why, the Vanderbilts themselves ain't in it any more—the people are too busy with us.

It's simply amazing what a difference one day may make. I think a complete change has come over me, and no wonder! It is enough to make any one mad the way they treat the girls, as if a body mustn't talk to anybody on the street. That's just why they've arrested Ray. It's ridiculous, their saying that she wanted to hit big Moe, as if that ruffian would be afraid of her. Poor kid, I'm real sorry for her, she has a hard lot with that whole family upon her frail shoulders, an' I don't see how she can do it. Here am I that ain't got any board to pay, for ma don't need my money. Pa makes enough to keep the whole lot of us, so whatever I make is my own, but a body needs a whole lot these days and I don't get much left out of my wages.

That's just the reason why I went down, just for the fun of it, but it's getting quite serious. I've come to believe that this strike business is something like a catching sickness—measles or chicken-pox. Once you get it it sticks to you until it's all over.

And then again, one can't really help standing up for the girls. I went down to see Minnie; she's down in bed; some hoodlum hit her last night. God! how those people do live! I don't see how she can afford to stop for a single day.

Her brother Mack is out of work, her father never works, Minnie and her sister, Sarah, are out on strike. Talk about nerve, I really think them Jew girls have it all. I'd like a share of it myself, but somehow I ain't of the brave kind. Ray said she'd rather starve to death than be a scab and take some one else's bread out of their mouths. I'm sure I couldn't have that much courage, but I'd hate to go back on the girls.

One of these talking women was trying to tell us girls that we ought to be glad of the opportunity to be idle for awhile—it gives us a chance to see and learn things that we could have never known anything about. She may be right, after all; what I've learned in these last two days is enough to put me wise to many a wrong. Only a little while ago I would have laughed had somebody told me that I would take this strike in earnest, but this afternoon, listening to the stories of assault upon the girls, watching the poor, miserable creatures that don't earn enough to keep body and soul together, I believe I was as much excited as the rest of them.

The girls said that Hayman is just furious because he can't get any scabs, and he wanted to make us believe that he's got more hands willing to work than he had work for. I wonder who was the first to use the name scab? By Jove, it's the right one at that; nobody clean could be mean enough to step into somebody else's shoes.

That was a pretty smart woman who said that the trouble with us girls is our seeing life from its funny side only. That we think it nothing but a place of entertainment and therefore try to dance through it. Then she added that it wasn't so—that life was a pretty serious proposition, and us girls should take our time to think more about it.

Honestly, there's nothing that will make you think so much as a strike does. I know it did me. I've been thinking and thinking till my head aches and when I think of meeting Jim my heart just goes way down to my boots, for I'm sure he'll say I've gone mad. And I like Jim better than I do anybody or anything in this world.

November 25

Another day spent in that dingy, smelly hall and still no end. Mr. Hayman don't come around and I'm pretty sure he won't come, either. The crowds increase every hour. Just like the ocean tide, their number grew higher and yet they said down at the headquarters that forty-one bosses have settled already and seven thousand girls are back to work. But then there are still four times seven thousand out and if the bosses will be settling at the rate of seven thousand in three days it will take almost two weeks before this big strike is settled. I think it's terrible. Why, some of the girls can't wait a day!

They asked me to go picketing, but I refused, of course. The idea of walking around the street corner as if I was a watch dog! They ought to be glad that I come down to their meetings every day. That ain't so bad; why, I even had a dance there this afternoon. And why not? A body may as well enjoy life if there's a chance.

I was kind of upset by what the last speaker said to us. According to her notion the bosses consider us nothing but hands and don't care what happens to us. It was simply humiliating to listen to her string of words, but when I come to think of it she was right, after all. If I'm out of a job and pick up a newspaper to look for work I go for the page where it says "hands wanted." If I'm delayed and come too late the boss informs me that he has all the hands he needs. And that's exactly what the woman said. It isn't the mother's daughter, or brother's sister, or Miss So-and-So that the boss wants, but a good, swift pair of hands, and, if they're used up, he looks for others. We don't count at all.

But that's a measly shame; we ought to put a stop to it! They say that the union will. If it should be true I vouch to stick to it. But who can believe everything they say! Not I. I guess I'll have to listen more carefully to their talking and find out things for myself. Oh, Lord! I'm so tired, and yet I didn't do a stitch of work for the last three days. I guess it's the excitement. To be sure, I'm having plenty of it. Jim was up here a little while ago. It's just as I had expected; why, he is just wild at my having mixed myself up with the strike. He said that I'd better quit and I said I won't, and before long we were having a tongue lashing and came pretty near having a falling out. That never happened to us since we have been going together.

The idea of his saying that a strike is good enough for these East Side girls, but he can't see the sense of my going into it. As if I was something better, made of different clay, perhaps. No, the speaker justly said that it makes no difference to what nationality we girls belong, or of what religion we are, so long as we have to work one is as good as the other, for all have one and the same interest—to make life a bit easier.

I'm mighty glad I had the courage to tell Jim just what I thought of his words. I'm sure he'll mind his business after this and I'll try to mind my own. It's a bit too much, him acting as if he is my boss already. Not by a long shot! There's many a slip between the cup and the lip.

Of course, I felt miserable when he left. This quarrel went like a shot through me. Jim can't even guess how much I love him, for I won't show him that I take it so much to heart. What's the use, he'll only get stuck up; they all do.

I suppose he thought I was one of them fickle kind that change their mind like some people their gloves. Well, let him, it'll all come out in the wash.

I ain't the only one to make sacrifices. Look at Minnie; she was engaged to be married and left man and all to come over here to help out her family. To tell the truth, one can't help being less selfish when a body is all the time with those noble Jew girls. During the day I'm usually so busy thinking of the strike that I often forget about Jim, for he is, after all, only one and they're so many, these poor suffering creatures. They are surely tired of this constant insult and abuse.

Well, as long as there is life there's hope; we'll see what the morrow has in store for us.

November 26

How some people do contradict themselves. Here's Mr. Hayman furious because the girls have made up their minds to form a union. And what does he do but go to work and organize one himself. Come to think of it, he had always been doing things that were tabooed to us girls.

It's strange, though; why should our bosses have to organize a union to fight us? Can't they do it single handed? They've lots of money, own the factories and machines. But no, they must needs come together in order to put up a fight against frail, poor, defenseless girls.

One of the speakers compared us the other day to a crowd of children out on the green playing a game of "London Bridge's Falling Down." The way she brought it out, it was self-understood that if us working girls will stand together and pull with all our might in the same direction we'll be sure to win. Our bosses will not be able to do anything against us then, not even if they all come together, for we will still have the numbers on our side. And I'm beginning to think that numbers count even more in real life than they do in games.

No doubt it will take some time before us girls can make them give in to us. The bosses have always been that proud—something better than us. And now we have cheek enough to stand up on our legs and demand that they come to the union to sign an agreement. Upon my word, we ought to be glad that we went out on strike—it teaches us self-respect.

If only the girls wouldn't be hounded so much. It's terrible the way they are treated, and what surprises me most is that they take it all. They seem to turn a deaf ear to everything. Their enthusiasm even grows with the hardships they're encountering. I think I'll try my hand at picketing tomorrow.

It ain't only our girls that are out doing the job, there is a lot of college women, members of the Woman's Trade Union League, who spend their days watching our factories. And a fine lot of women they are at that. I've come to know quite a number of them. What sets me a thinking is the fact that these women could go on living to their heart's content. They needn't come downtown among us if they don't want to, and why should they do it? It can't be for the sake of what's in it, for there ain't much fun in standing around the bleak, cold corners, being arrested by the cops and taken to the station house and police court.

I shouldn't wonder that their conscience pricks them a bit— they must be ashamed of being fortune children while so many of the girls have never known what a good day means. The rich women seem to be softer than the men; perhaps it's because they ain't making the money—they're only spending it. Or is it that women, as a rule, are better natured than their men folk? The saying has it that there is nothing so bad as a bad woman, nor anything better than a good one. I must admit the league women are the goodest of the good. And the Woman's Trade Union League in general is a mighty good thing for us girls.

Sarah was crying bitterly this afternoon, and I don't wonder. The idea of Mr. Hayman calling her a street woman! He surely knows better. Why, she has always been the quietest and most refined girl in the workroom. It's just because she's a foreigner. I'm sure he wouldn't dare say that to me. He knows that I wouldn't stand for it. I'd simply take the law into my own hands. And let him try to arrest me if he will.

It's really too bad that the strikers are mostly foreigners. Somehow everybody thinks that they can be handled in any which way and this is just the reason why the cops and the judges are so free in abusing and punishing them so much, when by rights they shouldn't be at all molested. The girls are attending to their own business, getting all the members they can to join the union. But the police ain't; they are sent to keep the peace and what do they do but start a row by using their big sticks on the girls' heads.

And our newspapers all seem to be tongue-tied! Not one of them dares to tell the truth of what is going on. And yet they ain't so dull. I suppose they wish to keep on the good side of our bosses.

November 27

I felt a bit shaky when I came down town this morning. But picketing ain't half as bad as I thought it would be. And another thing—it's enough to get down in that neighborhood and see the way these cops handle our girls, to be mad through and through; there ain't no thought of shame in them.

To tell the truth—it's only false pride—this imaginary shame is. There is nothing dishonest in standing up for one's bread. We must warn the newcomers that us girls are out on strike because our boss is paying starvation wages. To be sure, this is a business of much consequence, and so far as I can see the union is really the one to help us out. Then why be ashamed to belong to it and fight for it? In fact, we're all union people, only we don't seem to remember it. This land is one big union, and us children were taught very early that united we stand and divided we fall, and that's just what we girls are demanding—the right to be united.

It's terrible, this "don't care" attitude towards us girls. We must do something to make the people realize the true condition. Poor girls! I don't blame them for having heavy hearts—

I'm only surprised that they don't weep tears of blood upon seeing the suffering of their dear ones.

No wonder they are so determined to win this battle—they couldn't continue in the old way any longer. A few days with them and their real troubles convinced me of it. The most of them are so pale and worn, as if they are too weak for anything.

And to think of it—they're accused of assaulting those thugs. But, to be sure, we have our fun with those cops; at least, I had this morning. Ray and I were walking about near Hayman's shop too frightened to say much to anybody—I, because it was my first spiel, and Ray, because she had a taste of the patrol wagon. When suddenly to our great joy we saw dainty little Violet coming along, her hands deep in her pockets, her beaver hat a bit to the side and an angelic smile on her red lips.

Just before she reached us she spied a strange girl coming towards Hayman's place, and immediately stopped to talk to her. She wasn't at it very long when a cop appeared on the scene, as if he had sprung up from under the ground. But Violet didn't seem to mind him a bit and went on tellin' the girl all about the strike. I must say she's the bravest of the brave, Violet is. Day in and day out, shivering from cold and at times drenched to the very skin, she is out and about helping us girls, for she herself ain't a worker.

"Move on!" says the cop to her angrily.

"I will when I'm through," she snapped at him bravely. Then added: "You can arrest me, if your want."

"Oh, you uptown scum!" spit out the cop. He had had his hands full with her before this, and walked off without another word. We had a good laugh at him, while Violet marched off with the girl to join the union.

Ray and I stayed out until after 12 o'clock. Make believe we weren't frozen when we got back. I went in to a lunch room and got a cup of hot coffee, but Ray didn't get even that much. She wouldn't think of spending 10 cents now-a-days, and do what I may she would not let me treat her. One would never think that there's so much pride in these little Jew girls. They always stand on their dignity as if they were still God's choen people.

I'm awfully tired and have a splitting headache, but still and all, I didn't have the blues the whole week long. Perhaps it's because real worries drive all the small ones away. If I had had such quarrels with Jim at any other time as I did for the past few days, I'd be sure to cry my eyes out from aggravation. Jim is just set on seeing me leave the strike, and I'm just as set on sticking to it. He even went so far as to threaten me—said that I'd have to make my choice. And suppose I will, I'm sure it's better to suffer than turn traitor, and this is just what I would be were I to leave the girls now, when they are abused the most, and treated worse than street dogs. Much as I love Jim, I'm beginning to see that he ain't perfect in every respect. If he was he wouldn't talk so coolly about our affair—yes, it's ours, mine as much as the others.

November 28

I stayed home today; thought I'd rest up a bit, but nothing doing—had more trouble than I've bargained for. Pa didn't have a chance to say much to me during the week; in fact, we hardly see him at all except Sundays and holidays. And I guess he had it in for me all along. At any rate, I got all that's a-coming to me today.

"See here," was the first thing he said to me this morning. "I've never been very strict with you girls; you've always had enough rope to run about, but not too much. I won't stand for it. I wouldn't have my neighbors point their finger at me. I ain't the kind to be pitied. You've been fooling around long enough with that strike business of your'n, and now it's high time to quit. I don't give a snap about the money you've lost during the week. It ain't that. It's just because I don't think it's a woman's place to be hangin' around street corners, fighting with rowdies and be taken to jail. Union is all good and well by itself, but it was never meant for the women."

His words just set my blood a boiling—as if it is woman's place to go out of the home in order to be the breadwinner for the family. If she's good enough to spend her days in some of the shops that ain't fit for pig stys, she may as well stand up on the corners and fight for her rights. I'm sure it's much better than standing on the corner for other purposes, which some women are compelled to do. And if woman is to go on submitting to the love-making of every rowdy that's got some power over her, she may as well teach others that she, too, can stand up for herself. I wouldn't have minded him so much, if he hadn't been a union man himself. People laugh at woman's reason, but, honestly, I think man's beats it all to pieces. Where's the difference between man and woman when it comes to work? They're both anxious to earn an honest living and have the right to protect themselves as best they can.

By this time my father had worked himself up to a point where he was sure to pitch into me, so I preferred to skip into the other room. Jim came in soon after and, of course, added more fuel to the fire. He hinted to pa that he ought to stop me from going down town, and immediately began to talk about our marriage. He knew that pa would be only too glad to get me off his hands. I heard every word they said, for I listened through the keyhole. See, Jim's mortally afraid that I'll remain a rebel even after I'm married.

Tired of listening any longer to their talk, I walked straight into the room and shook hands with Jim as if nothing had happened. I think he cares for me in his own foolish way, for he noticed the change in me immediately:

"What ails you, Mary?" he exclaimed uneasily. My face was all afire, but my hands were as cold as ice. Pa, too, saw my condition and didn't say another word. But everybody felt rather out of sorts, so I suggested to Jim that we take a walk.

It's strange how often we find ourselves in the most ridiculous position. Here we were walking side by side, Jim and I, each just bubbling over with emotion and yet—neither dared to touch upon the subject uppermost in his mind.

It is pretty tough on a girl to be striking, quarrel with her family, and be on the outs with her beau all at the same time. What gets me is his saying that I'm out of place there, for I personally don't feel the suffering. As if a body can go through life thinking of nothing but self. And another thing, he harps on the fact that I'm about to be married. Well! I don't know as I am, but suppose it was so! Does he really imagine that I'll be dead to everything else?

I don't really know why, but somehow I think that this strike has brought trouble for the two of us. Why we've walked for nigh two hours this afternoon, and it was precious little that we had to say to one another. To tell the truth, I didn't know what to say to him. So long as we were both satisfied with talking nonsense, we used to go around fooling each other for hours. But now I'm beginning to think that Jim don't really know very much. At any rate we've parted in a worse mood than we met.

November 29

When I think that a whole week has passed since I have joined this big army I must smile at myself. I first looked upon the whole thing as a new sort of amusement and was sure that I'd tire of it before long, but now I realize that I've become a part and parcel of it.

Here I've been standing for more than a half a day picketing, was chilled to the very bone, came pretty near being arrested, but it all doesn't seem to matter—I'm ready to do it over again tomorrow. And no wonder! It is enough to arouse the dead from their graves, this horrible treatment of the girls. Upon my word the judges and cops act as if we were some obnoxious insects that crawl under their feet and try to crush us. People talk about Russia as the place of darkness and persecution! I honestly believe that nothing worse could be going on there.

If only the girls had been prepared for it all, but they weren't. Most of them were still penniless from the dull summer season and didn't even have a chance to buy some warm clothes. It's simply heartbreaking to see them out on the streets in their short little jackets or sweaters. I gave Rose my coat this afternoon, for it was terribly cold out, and as luck would have it, the poor kid was arrested and kept in the station house, so I had to go home in her sweater. A good thing I got in without ma seeing me, or she would have made a big fuss about it.

But I really think it's wonderful the way these Jew girls go at it. Hungry, tired and cold, it doesn't seem to matter, their enthusiasm grows with their hardships. And yet—why should I be surprised at them, when I'm about the same—I've come to think that the more danger there's in being arrested, the more eager I am to do my duty. Perhaps, it's because I'd like to show the cops and everybody else that the Jew girls aren't the only brave and sensible ones—us Americans are beginning to see a thing or two, which is bound to knock the foolish pride out of us. We, too, can stand up for a principle.

The affair about Max, who worked for Goldstein's, just touched me to the quick—the fellow was the shop chairman and turned scab. "Don't judge and thou shalt not be judged," my Sunday school teacher often said to me, and there's a great deal of truth to it. Max isn't so much to blame after all. He was without a cent to his name, his baby took sick and another one was coming any day. When the man was almost out of his wits from despair, Mr. Goldstein came to his house, gave him twenty-five dollars in cash and promised to see him through all his troubles.

Who would be strong enough to turn away such an offer? It is easier to go cold and hungry than to hear the little ones moan and beg for bread. I know I could never stand it and, to tell the truth, I can't imagine how any parent is able to go on working and believing while the children starve to death.

That's just why we oughtn't to blame the poor scabs so much. I think they deserve more pity than anything else, for they're still blind to the truth. But on the other hand, some of them scabs are so darn stupid and pig-headed that it doesn't do them any harm to get a licking once in a while.

The worst part is that the wrong ones are sure to be punished—we've had twenty arrests today and, as luck would have it, the most helpless and timid were among those caught. And it's always the case, it seems, that people have either too much sunshine in their lives or none at all. I think life is a funny game as it goes on now-a-days. Somehow it doesn't seem right. Here are those ladies that come around to look at us—they idle their time away with nothin' and it makes me real mad, when they try to tell us that it ain't lady-like to go out on strike. Why don't they say that it ain't lady-like to go out into the factories and work from morn until night and the same thing over again the next day till we get to see nothing but work and the machine before us. I'd just like to put them for a few hours and make them turn the wheel as swift as we have to do it. But they never did it and don't think they ever will either.

November 30

It's funny, but some of us seem to be entitled to privileges just because we happen to be born in a certain place. Here am I, who knows perhaps less than a good many of the other girls, and just because I'm an American they try to push me forward all the time.

This morning I had to go and see the Mayor. There were other big guys with me, but I guess I would have never had that chance if it wasn't for the strike. To confess the truth, I saw no sense of going—what's the use, as though he don't know everything that's going on in his own city. What sort of a city keeper would he be if he didn't? But what I think is even worse than his not knowing it, is his not caring a snap as to what happens to us girls.

The Mayor kept us waiting in the office for a good long while before he chose to come in. True enough, he was as sweet as pie to us. But I'm sure that's where it will all end, for he won't do more for us now than he did before. I don't pretend to know much about politics and never care to be a labor leader, but I'd be blessed if I'd ever advise anybody to go and beg of those that ain't anxious to give of their own free will.

I felt like a fool when I left that place, and was simply disgusted with the manner in which some of them big guys cringed before him. Why should they?—he's nothing but a plain, ordinary person, perhaps, even worse than some of us, only that he had a chance to get a good fat job. And now that he's got it and his wife and children have plenty of everything he don't care about us that ain't got it. And he ain't the only one, either; there were a lot of big fat hogs hanging around there in the corridors, just smoking their cigars and doing nothing, while out on the streets thousands of innocent girls are being punished for wanting to earn an honest living.

Oh, it's just terrible, this utter helplessness. I do wish I could do something for the poor and miserable. I don't see really how the rich can be so heartless—is money everything after all? I know that I don't seem to care for it lately, except when I came into the Bloom house this morning and saw Rose prostrated in bed, the kid was badly beaten, besides being arrested. And the brood of little ones crying from cold and hunger, the mother being away to do a day's washing for somebody. It's only then that I wished I had lots and lots of money that I might make their lot a bit easier.

Talk about martyrs, I guess Rose is the real stuff. Here she is the supporter of the family ever since her father died three years ago, leaving five children, herself the oldest.

I told their story to the Mayor, all except that I had thirty cents, twenty-five of which I spent for coal and bread for them. Your Honor, said I, it's terrible to see their suffering at any time, and here is she who's supporting them laid up in bed, and the Lord knows when she'll be able to earn another cent. I simply couldn't go on any more and began to cry, for I felt as though my heart would break. But a lot he cared, all he said was: "My child, there is no use of getting excited over it. We will look into the matter and try to punish the guilty."

Yes, I believe him—we will be the guilty party and he'll surely punish us. What galls me most is this constant cry—that girls shouldn't be striking. And why shouldn't the girls go out on strike? Have they no eyes to see that they are being abused? No reason, no senses, no feelings to be hurt? When they go wrong aren't they punished, and when they are wronged shouldn't they try to defend themselves? Is it a crime to tell the boss: "You've insulted, abused us and taken away the bigger part of our hard earned money, while we worked on in silence, but now the tables are turned, sir, you've taught us by your own behavior how to deal with you hereafter"?

I really think it's high time that people stop shaking their heads about our doings. For it's but few that look cheery at us. And yet it don't prevent me from having bright hopes for the future. At any rate we learn more and more as we go along, and that counts.

December 1

People say that a new month is sure to bring new luck with it, but I fail to see it in our case. The fight is now worse than ever; though many of the bosses have settled there are still so many strikers that one imagines they grow over night.

As the days go by the girls suffer more and more. During the tedious picket duty they get frozen, catch colds, go without food until they're nothing but shadows of their former selves—it's real disheartening.

When I got down to the headquarters this morning I had to go and help out at the information bureau. Lord! complaints were coming in faster than I could put them down.

"A ruffian tore my coat and broke my glasses," cried a girl at the top of her voice. "I haven't another coat and can't make a step without the glasses."

"Be glad it ain't your head," consoled another whose face and eyes were swollen and bruised. She told me later that she was beaten by a thug while out on picket duty.

"I got no more hair," complained a third one. "Tim that works by Cohen, he pulls them all out of me."

"Ach Got, mein Got!" pleaded a stooping man with a long, unkempt beard streaked with gray. "Mine children, they hungry. I want one job."

It almost broke my heart to listen to his plea. I think it's a shame that a man of his age should have to work and go out on strike. But it seemed rather strange—the man knew his children were hungry and that he could get work if he wouldn't be so scrupulous and become a scab. But I really admire him more than blame him.

"I'm that mad I can't see straight!" assured me a girl of about sixteen. "I stay out until 4 o'clock this morning in the night court—close to a lot of drunken bums and street women. I know the judge; he do it for spite; he just loves us poor people. And when I got home my ma gave me terrible scolding; she didn't believe I was in court. She thinks I was fooling around somewhere."

I was dreadfully excited by that girl's story. One could scarcely believe that men with families of their own would be so deaf to all sense of justice. Who could blame this young girl if she would go wrong?

"Hey, children, children, I say nothin'," murmured an old, toothless woman, her wrinkled face propped up with both hands. "I make $5 one week to keep myself and my two childs. The girls in my shop they go on strike. I no stay one scab. But it's bad; my children they no eat nothin' today."

Five dollars a week for three people! How is it possible? What sort of a life must they lead? I must admit that I'm beaten. I've always thought that I was bad off—but Lord! we live in perfect bliss in comparison to this woman and many others like her. I'm just beginning to find out what real misery means. It's simply dreadful—dreadful is hardly strong enough a word for it. And people wonder why we are out striking! The only thing that takes me is the bravery of the girls—one would think that this sort of life ought to crush every bit of energy in them, but it doesn't look it. I guess their energy thrives on suffering; it seems to grow with it.

Why! this one day at the information bureau broke me up completely, I could almost write a whole book from the tales I heard and sights I saw there. I felt like dazed on going home and when I got there I found Jim waiting for me. I forgot all about that this was Wednesday night—beau's night. Jim thought it wasn't proper for me to stay down town so late, that the day was long enough for this tomfoolery and that I'm getting to be as lawless as one of them darn anarchists. Just for the fun of it I'd like to meet one of them and see if they're really as black as they're painted. For it seems that Jim can't find anything worse to compare me with. And yet—I doubt if he knows what an anarchist is like—it can't be that he does, or he wouldn't call us girls anarchists. If the people at large weren't worse than us girls it would, perhaps, be easier to live in this cold, merciless world.

And it wasn't all in words, either, my falling out with Jim, for there were others around; it's our looks that told more than the words.

December 2

I was so tired last night that I left the sitting room before Jim was gone and this morning Ma informed me that they had talked it all over—that is, Jim and Pa, for Ma ain't got much to say when Pa's around.

Funny—they've decided my fate for me. I'm to quit going down town, Jim to try and rush things up for our marriage and Pa'll manage to keep me in clothes for the time being, until Jim'll take me off his hands.

And they are considered sensible men! What did they think? I was their baggage, perhaps. It must be so, or they could never have thought that they had a right to dispose of me at their own sweet will. I wonder if they thought of keeping me under lock and key or permit me at large?

To think of it—just because I happened to be born a woman! Well, what of it? Ain't I of the same flesh and bone as a man? I, too, was carried under a mother's heart. And since I was born I've suffered from almost the same diseases and was healed by exactly the same medicines. I walk under the same sky and tread the same earth as men do. I, too, have senses, moods and reasons, am old enough to judge for myself; but they didn't seem to think so. Well, I must say—they've made the mistake of their life if they think that I'll abide by their resolution.

Of course, even while Ma was telling me all about last night's conference I was getting ready to go down town. But I couldn't help thinking of it until I got to the meeting rooms. Here they're talking of my marriage to Jim when I'm just commencing to think that we don't even know each other well enough. That is, I've come to think so of late, for it seems to me that he ain't the Jim I took him for. I disagree more and more with him and am shocked at times at his ignorance of things that concern everyday life. And what is even worse than his ignorance is the fact that he thinks he knows it all and I ought simply listen to what he tells me.

Well, this was certainly the day for feeling blue—it poured cats and dogs, as if nature itself was sympathizing with me. But I forgot myself as soon as I came face to face with the bigger sorrow. And I don't see how anybody can look into the gulf on the brink of which our girls are standing without feeling a pang of keenest grief, without a desire to do something only to make their lot easier.

Poor devils! their worn clothes and torn shoes were just soaked by the peltering rain. To tell the truth, we were all a sorry sight to look at—the dirty water pouring from the hats down upon the face and neck. But even then I couldn't help laughing at Annie's beaver hat; it looked too funny for anything—all shriveled up and out of shape. This lasted only a moment for I bethought myself that it is the only hat she has and may not be able to buy another this winter.

I think that even the cops pitied us this morning, while some old gentleman offered to buy us rubbers. The girls refused his offer, but I've been wondering whether he really meant it out of the goodness of his heart or was it some new scheme to trap us girls.

Everybody tried to make love to the little coal stove when we got back to the meeting rooms. But I wouldn't be a bit surprised if many of the girls will be laid up with sore throats by tomorrow. It is terrible; they go down like flies. There's scarcely a shop but has a number of girls sick in bed. This makes it so much harder for those who are still up. Poor Ray, her teeth were just rattling when she got back this afternoon; even the cup of hot water we gave her didn't help much. She ain't fit to work or strike, either. It's a sanitarium and good care that she needs, but where is she to get it, and what will the others do without her?

How is it that people walk around with their eyes open and yet don't seem to see all these things?

December 3

Well, well, this was one of the busy days. Have been on the go since early in the morning. But I don't mind it a bit; we've had one of the finest parades I ever saw. We went to the Mayor's office, but—to tell the truth—it wasn't so much for what the Mayor may do for us as to let the people see for themselves of whom this strike is made up—mostly children more fit for the school room than the shop. But these very children have to work good and hard, and for starvation wages at that.

But to come back to the parade—we, that is, mostly the League women, thought of it first yesterday about 4 o'clock in the afternoon. But it didn't matter, these people act instead of talking. Half-past 4 Ida and I were down at the Commissioner's office and got our permit. From there we rode over to a painter's and ordered the placards delivered at the theater at noon today. Then we rushed down to a couple of newspapers and got them to put in the announcement. From there we went to the headquarters, notified the people and appointed some of our committees. By this time it was getting pretty late, so we went home and early this morning a half dozen of us started out to make the round among the different meeting halls, urging the girls to be on hand for the parade.

When I got back to my shop meeting I just had enough time to eat a pretzel and a piece of chocolate—had to rush off to the theater where the parade was to start. It just made my hair stand up on my head when the girls came forward and told about some of the abuses they had suffered at the hands of the police. I believe the bosses must pay a big booty to these cops. It did my heart good when the speaker up to the theater turned to the police present and said: "Why don't you go out and fight rascals of your own size instead of these little girls; there're plenty of them in this big city."

I'm inclined to believe that the cops must have tough shoe leather instead of hearts in their body, or they could never be as brutal as they are now. What security have they that their own daughters would not have to work for a living some day? I think it's perfectly true what the speaker said—it's nothing but poor wages that drives a girl on the street. Imagine some of them making $3 and $4 a week and nobody to help them out in dull season. But our girls are as good as gold. I could almost vouch for every one of them.

The meeting didn't last long. About half-past 1 there were ten thousand girls in line ready to tell the boss of the City Hall and the rest of us that they're willing to work, provided they are paid enough to make an honest living and that if he is true to his oath he ought to put a stop to the antics of all those hoodlums that abuse us girls on every step.

It's strange what silly notions some of us would have—I remember once long ago we watched a number of women taking part in a labor day parade. Well, we thought it the funniest thing out and called after them "Coxey's Army!" and many other things. But you never can tell what changes may come over us—here I was, a real born American, marching in broad daylight through the Bowery, a big sign in hand and as proud as I could be, for I was on my way to stand up for my rights, and didn't our forefathers stand up for theirs! They not only marched through the Bowery, but fought on it.

I can imagine, though, what Jim would have to say if he saw me in that crowd and heard some of the remarks that the people on the sidewalks passed about us. As if anybody cares! Let them laugh—he laughs best who laughs last, and the end hasn't come yet; these people are bound to wake up some day, even as I did during this strike.

Of course, it was just as I thought it would be—the Mayor accepted our committee, listened to its tale of woe, shook his head and promised to look into the matter. I guess he is as bad as the cops—for they wouldn't dare to act the way they do if they weren't aware that he approves of it. It was funny to see the few men among us, but I give them credit for coming out; they were braver than the cowards who remained at the meeting halls.

People told me that it was the most dignified parade that had ever passed in that neighborhood.

December 4

These are days of excitement—yesterday the parade, tomorrow the Hippodrome meeting. I wonder what next. The girls were just wild about tomorrow's affair; you could hear them talk of nothing else but Mrs. Belmont; they've even forgot their own troubles for a while. It is rather strange, her offering to pay for the big place. I wonder what made her do it? She must surely be better than the rest of her kind if she is willing to spend her money to help us girls rather than give a monkey dinner or buy a couple of new pet dogs.

But then, why shouldn't she? She's got plenty of money. And to think how much the papers make of her. I think that she and the rest of her kind ought to be thankful to us girls for giving them a chance to do a good deed. I know I felt fine when I spent my last quarter for the Bloom kids, and Mrs. Belmont doesn't have to give her last, I am sure.

In a way I think it's really a shame that the very rich get so much free advertising while little Violet and many others like her, who are really sacrificing themselves to help us out, shouldn't be mentioned at all, except when they are arrested and taken to jail.

Stopped on the square this afternoon and listened to them that talks votes for women. It's all very true. I also say that a woman is every bit as good as a man and should have the same rights with him. But us girls have something else to think of just now. We must see to it that we win the strike for bread and then we can start one for the ballot.

As I was leaving the square I met a girl going to the head-quarters; her face was all swollen, one of her teeth knocked out, her clothes in tatters and she running around since early this morning unable to find a policeman willing to arrest the brute who beat her so terribly. I wonder if this is what our good Mayor is doing for us?

As I said, we have our hands full just at present—a number of girls went back on us. The fools got scared because Hayman told them that he'd rather go out of business than give in to us girls. I don't believe a word he says—what else would he do if not be in business unless he turned dog catcher? But it wouldn't pay as well as the waist making business does.

The pity of it is that us working people don't really realize what a power we are. I fully agree with that speaker who said that in spite of all their money our bosses couldn't get along without us working people. For if they had even a hundred times as many machines, and the whole world built of factories, they couldn't deliver a single order unless the working people chose to make them up.

But how are the girls to know all these things? I'm sure not by sitting day in and day out at the machine, rushing, pushing and hustling all in order to make another couple of cents. And one can't blame them for doing it; it's precious little they make, even at that.

The Lord knows that they're near enough to starvation. The worst part of it is that very few can realize what it means to lead a life like the most of our girls are leading. For somehow it seems to me that if the people would really know the true state of affairs, if they could be brought to realize that the girls have ventured out on this strike because they can't stand it any longer, they wouldn't remain quietly at their comfortable homes while thousands of girls are being driven to the dogs.

The papers say that Mrs. Belmont is worth millions; that each of her hats and suits is worth hundreds of dollars. If this be true and if she is affected by the girls' sufferings, why doesn't she try to do something more for us. If she really feels about it the way I do why don't she come down among us, feed the hungry and warm the cold? I didn't see her even once and I don't believe any of the girls did. Perhaps she thinks she's too high-toned to come down here. Well, then, she can just stay where she is, and us girls will try to fight our own battles. I'm anxious to have a look at her tomorrow.

December 5

Lord! I never saw anything like it in my life—that Hippodrome meeting. The place was so crowded that I had trouble in getting in, though I did come rather early. But once I was in it was worth all the trouble of getting there. It did my heart good to see how happy every one of our girls looked. There, more than in any other place, I felt the kinship between all the girls and myself. It seemed to me that their joy was my joy, their sorrow my own. It seemed as if I had grown a pair of wings that lifted me nearer to heaven. I sang and laughed, and was happy like all the rest of them. For I felt as though I had been born anew and became a power. I knew that if I should happen to be hurt or abused all these thousands of men and women would stretch out their hands to lift me out of danger.

It is really a wonderful feeling that comes over one when a body finds itself surrounded by thousands of people all assembled for the same purpose, breathing the same hopes and thinking the same thoughts—it's like an immense giant born for the purpose of doing justice to all.

I think the speaker must have felt the same way when she said that one person in himself is something like a lone tree planted in a desert. It is bound to wither and die under the steady burning of the hot sun and the heavy gales of wind. But all the people united together are like a great shady forest where every tree, small or large, is protected by all the others, so that all have their chance to grow and prosper. Yes, when I come to think of it I realize that one person by himself, no matter how rich or clever he may be, can't exist very long, unless he is helped and protected by everybody else.

It is strange, that I've lived for over twenty years, gone through school and Sunday school and never gave it a thought until to-day. I'm beginning to think that this strike is the best thing that could have happened to me, though it may cost me Jim's love.

He was with me at the meeting and said that I've surely gone crazy, the way I behaved down there. I believe he was touched to the quick by the votes for women speaker—she said that woman, married or unmarried, has as much right to live and enjoy life as any man. That the women are foolish to permit themselves to be ruled and patronized by men.

"I can see my finish," snapped Jim at me when we left the place. "I guess I'll have to quit if you continue to keep company with these loons."

And mighty sane loons they are at that. I wonder if Jim ever heard a talk that had more common sense in it than he did this afternoon at the Hippodrome. But as the saying goes, none are so deaf as those that will not hear. He thought he'll scare me by his warning. A lot I care! What is my little trouble compared with the suffering of the great big forest of people?

I was anxious to see Mrs. Belmont, but the meeting proved so interesting that I forgot all about her. To tell the truth—I ain't got much use for these rich, especially since I've learned how miserable the poor are. Somehow I can't believe they are human—if they were they couldn't stand for all this misery.

The most of our girls had to walk both ways in order to save their car fare. Many came without dinner, but the collection baskets had more pennies than anything else in them—it was our girls themselves who helped to make it up, and yet there were so many rich women present. And I'm sure the speakers made it plain to them how badly the money is needed, then how comes it that out of the $300 collected there should be $70 in pennies?

I'm sorry I couldn't help with the collection. Jim wouldn't let me. I could have found out for myself just who gave the most. Make believe I wasn't furious at Jim, but what could I do? I wouldn't start a quarrel with him right there and then. But I'm afraid it's coming, this real quarrel is. All these little disagreements bode no good to either of us. We seem to be drifting apart daily. I often think it's a good thing that it all happened before we were married, for the Lord knows how it will all end.

December 6

Lord! my nerves are all on edge, but I'm glad that I read the law to her. The scab on the body, as a rule, comes from hunger and privation, but with Mame it is nothing but a case of sheer cussedness. She's just a mean, vile, paltry scab from scabby land!

Talk about the proud, independent American—I must admit I'm ashamed of my country-women; they're the worst scabs living. One can't really do a thing with them but beat it into their heads. Anybody that knows me knows that I ain't the kind to go in for a fist fight; in fact, I don't think I've every laid my hands on anybody before this, but I'm not a bit sorry for giving her that lesson; she needed it badly.

It seems almost incredible that she was my best friend once upon a time and that I was, in a way, as bad as she is today. And I'm mighty glad of the change; I wouldn't want to get back to her way of thinking for a fortune.

What set my blood a-boiling is the manner in which she commenced to yell as soon as Fanny and I came near her. This was a signal for that ruffian Ben to fall upon poor Fanny and pound her with all his might. And what could I do but lay it in to Mame, even if she had been my friend? In love and in war everything, they say, is fair.

Fanny's face is black and blue, her eyes are all swollen, but she won't hear of complaining against that hoodlum, for fear that they may get after me then. No wonder that Christ had sacrificed himself for all mankind; it seems to run in the Jewish blood, this spirit of self-sacrifice. But somehow I have a premonition that they'll get me just the same. It wouldn't be like Mr. Hayman to let a thing like that slip by.

The way they stick to their union, or make believe they do! I only wish our girls would be as wise as all that, but they ain't; they carry their troubles on their sleeves. When we started to discuss the strike this morning, some of the girls, and even more so the men, were for giving up the fight and going back without the union. I think these men of ours would surely take the first prize in cowardice. To think that they don't lift a finger to help win the strike, but are ready on the job when there's any kicking to be done. I had occasion to know some of the white trash that lives in the South, and, honestly, as I watch these so-called men of ours I can't help calling them— man-trash.

I was proud, though, of some of the girls and the fine arguments they've put up in favor of holding out. "What do we lose?" asked Minnie. "We've gone cold and hungry before this, and a little more or less won't matter. If we can afford to starve on the boss' account we can also afford to do it on our own; perhaps it will help in the long run; perhaps the sun will still shine even for us. I think we're entitled to a bit of it."

"If you had brains in your head instead of corn mush," admonished Ray, "you'd readily understand that if Mr. Hayman objects to having a union you ought to stick up for it. The bosses are smarter than us working people; they know that hundreds and thousands of girls and men bound together for the purpose of helping all are a terrible power, and, therefore, they are fighting this power and nothing else, but you people don't know your own strength; you're ready to cut your own throats. By urging us to give up the strike you're rushing to your doom. And all because you can't see farther than your nose, you're willingly shutting your eyes to the future."

"It's only lobsters that creep backward. People with common sense move on all the time. Lot's wife was changed into a mountain of salt for turning back, and you'll be sure to shed enough tears to make a salt lake," warned them Sarah.

"I ain't going back just the same," assured us Rose. "But Lord help those of you who do—we'll break every bone in your body."

So we argued and threatened and quarreled until we won— we ain't going back until we get a signed agreement. But who can foretell how it will all end? Hunger and want are pressing more and more upon the girls, their strength, too, is giving out, while the bosses are waging a more bitter fight than ever. But what's the use worrying?

December 7

I thought so—Mr. Hayman wasn't the kind to let things slip by—he went after me bright and early, as soon as I got near the shop. And now I'm a real striker—felt the grip of a policeman's hand, had a free ride in a patrol wagon, spent a few hours at the police station and was arraigned in court. One may imagine things, but not until you meet them face to face do you really know what they are like.

Not until I was placed in a real cell and the door shut behind me did I realize what it means to be a prisoner, to be deprived of freedom of action and speech. And yet—ain't we deprived of it every day of our lives, I mean us working girls? We go to the factory bright and early in the morning and after that until we leave we are practically prisoners, except that we don't know it and imagine that we are there of our own free will; but it ain't so, we are there because we must or we would starve.

This is, perhaps, one of the reasons that us girls don't mind the jail as much as other people do, for we're used to the filth and dirt and a good many other things. But what shocked me beyond words was the horrible behavior of the policemen. And they kept to protect us from harm!

"How late were you out last night?" asked one of them.

"Oh, I don't think she has caught him yet," chimed in another; "she's looking for a match right now."

"They are silly, these girls are," assured a third. "Where's the sense of their going on strike when a woman can earn plenty of money without working?"

It's sickening to repeat all the things they did say to us girls as we sat in our cells huddled in a corner, afraid to breathe or even look up, for their eyes were full of beastly poison.

I don't know what I looked like, but it was certainly a pity to watch the other girls—they were too scared for anything—on the one end the horrid policemen, on the other four drunken women. Every time the policemen said something nasty the women let out a shriek that could be heard two blocks away. Across the hall from us a man kept walking back and forth like a caged animal. The terrible look in his eyes made me think of the tigers in the park—it was enough to make anybody refrain from approaching him.

A good thing that the captain got word that another batch of strikers were coming and he had to make room for them, so he took our names, asked a whole lot of questions and gave us another free ride to the court house. And I was mighty glad at that—didn't have to go to the night court or tell anything about being a jailbird to the folks at home.

Now I always thought that a court house was a magnificent place where sits a grave, dignified judge, many clerks, stenographers and great lawyers. But what a sad disappointment—the place they brought us to wasn't much better than the station house. The judge looked as though he had been out on a spree. The lawyers—a lot of cheap guys that you see hanging around the corner saloons. And the audience—well, they beat it all! One could have made up a funny museum of them. And talk about cases—a husband charged with licking his wife; a German woman accused of pouring out the leavings upon her neighbor; a wife deserter, a pickpocket, a drunken woman, a sneak thief, a dozen or more strikers.

One couldn't really recall them all. What I'm wondering at is how Miss Elizabeth could stand it all—to be there day in and day out and she not striking, either, except against everything that's wrong.

I thought it rather silly when they made me swear that I'll tell the truth—everybody else swore to do it, but as far as I could judge, very few told the honest truth.

"Your honor," says I when my turn came. "I saw them fight with each other and I knew them all, so I stepped in and took them apart. I'm sure you would have done the same if you were there."

And he had to admit that he would, but it seemed so funny to him that he had to laugh right out. "Discharged," said he, "and try to keep out of my way."

December 8

Another wrinkle—a conference of all the arrested girls. I only wonder where they find names to all these different conferences, but, then, what is the difference? You learn something new every time.

But it really amounts to this: The League women saw at last there ain't no use sending committees to the Mayor, or telling our troubles to a policeman, so, to please the girls, they got us to tell our troubles to that good soul—Helen. Of course, we understand that she can't do much for us in that line, but if she'll only give us a few of her kind smiles it will make it easier to bear the burden. And of this we were pretty certain, for Helen has always a smile for us girls, even when her heart breaks from sorrow. It's my belief that the kind soul will go down to her grave with a smile on her lips.

And still and all, I was startled to see the room filled with girls, each eager to tell her tale of woe, but it did my heart good to see their temper of rebellion—every one of them was prepared to face the music to the bitter end. And if those that hound us had only been present they would have understood the folly of their policy of trying to subdue us by such outrageous treatment.

Why, it's hardly believable that all these girls were arrested in a free land, for no bigger crime than the desire to stand up for their rights. Talk about being anarchists—I really wonder if that name doesn't suit the police better than it does us girls? And my pa, a good union man, has the courage to say that it ain't a girl's place to belong to a union!

I just wondered this morning where the protectors of all these girls were hiding. It's on our own responsibility that our parents sent us out to hunt for a job, and get in and out of all sorts of traps—then what sort of a love can they have for us when they deny us the right to band together for mutual protection?

In a way, I think we girls are to blame for being so timid all along and now everybody got so used to it that they take it for granted—it must be so. But, I'm glad to say, we left off creeping, and if we can do this much at the first attempt we're sure to be able to stand on our feet before very long. Once your eyes are opened you can't help seeing and protesting against everything that's wrong. They might as well stop the incoming tide as stop a body from fighting for liberty to lead a decent life.

The judges and police make the mistake of their lives if they hope to stop us by keeping up this jail business—every new arrest makes a firm convert to the cause. The girls' sense of justice becomes sharpened by the fact that they are persecuted for telling the truth. Helen tried to assure us that they'll impeach the judges—I'd like to know who'll be brave enough to do it. But anything is good, so long as it quiets the girls.

Some of the League women rushed off in a hurry, they said, to hold a conference with the bosses. I do hope they'll come to some understanding this time, for this strike is just killing many of the girls. But some of them labor leaders needn't think that they can bunco us into any tom fool settlement, for we won't stand for it. Us girls have come to realize that the welfare of one means the welfare of all, and this is likewise true about the hardships. Annie and Rosie don't amount to anything as long as they remain only hands and stand up each one for herself and let the devil take the hindmost.

But there are a few sleek go-betweens, smooth-tongued spiders I'd call them, and it's them that's trying hard to entangle us girls into a net. One of them mistook me for somebody else this morning and said more than he would have had he known I was a striker. That's how I came to know that they would like the League women to sign an agreement with the bosses and declare the strike off without consulting us girls about it. I listened quietly to all he had to say and never said a word to contradict him—it's good to keep your views to yourself once in a while and somebody else's, too, for future reference.

December 9

I tell you, life seems to be made up of surprises, and I certainly had one this afternoon when I went down to a meeting at the Thalia Theater arranged by those Socialists. I heard of them before this, of course, but only when pa was very much disgruntled with his union, then he would come home and put all the blame for it on the Socialists, which made me think that they were the worst ever.

But it wasn't really the Socialists that attracted me to the meeting—I was curious to see that woman the papers have written so much about, the one everybody calls mother. I couldn't understand how she could be a mother to everybody when it's real hard to mother one's own family.

To be sure, I know better now. One glance into her glittering eyes, a glimpse at the noble face and outstretched arms that are anxious to embrace the whole human race, is enough to make you understand how she does it, not to say anything of the words of wisdom that flow from her lips.

And suppose she gives her whole time to help others—that's what I call worth while living for. She's as happy as she can be, and if I was to compare her with my mother I'd surely take the latter for the martyr. And the reason for it is probably the fact that we're but one great family after all; that is, all the people the world over, no matter what color we are or what religion we believe in, and it's the welfare of that big family that should by rights interest us first, for isn't the whole bigger than the part, and each small family is but a part of the big one.

I must say, what with all the things we see for ourselves, and the different speeches we hear, a body can't help getting new ideas; but I know Jim would be sure to say that I've graduated into an anarchist. Let him. I think our people smell a rat and are bound to let me know it pretty soon.

But coming back to the meeting—I've learned a great deal there. That two armies of fighting soldiers isn't the only war in existence; that there is a terrible war raging just now and I'm a soldier in that war and that is the war for a bit of bread. I suppose I've felt it for some time, only I couldn't reason it out for myself; it took the people's mother to do it.

I could see that we working people were standing by ourselves, while on the other side stood our bosses, also a bunch by themselves, and now the way Mother Jones explained it to us it is clear that our bosses can't have any love for us, for every time we make a cent more they have a cent less left for themselves, and every time they can squeeze an extra cent from us they're that much the gainer. And from what I've seen for the last few weeks with my own eyes I can't help realizing that they've become so hardened in their growing greed that they're just ready to fight us to the end.

The mother said that it didn't have to go on that way, that all of us could have enough to live on if we only managed our own affairs in the right way, and if this is what the Socialists teach I earnestly believe they're talking common sense.

If one has patience to listen to their string of talk it becomes self evident that they've certainly learned what ails the people nowadays, and, I suppose, that by understanding the injustice they were able to find a remedy. To tell the truth, I don't see what we working people have to lose by trying their way of management. We can't be much worse off than we are today, I'm sure.

And I think they've pretty good people among them. They say that the little Jew girl who married one of them millionaires, the lucky dog—well, she's a Socialist, and she's certainly been good to her kind, especially to us girls during the strike. Why, she don't think anything of coming right among us, as if she was still a working girl, and doing all sorts of jobs—nothing is too small or too hard for her. And here's brave Mother Jones and many of the other people who have been our best friends during this trouble, and, as the saying goes, a friend in need is a friend indeed.

As I said once before, if only us girls could bring ourselves to reason out things for ourselves.

December 10

I'm really surprised at myself and all the courage I'm working up. But I've come to think that heroes ain't born, but made by circumstances. When I got near Levinson's factory this morning it just made me wild to see that high iron fence put up in front of the entrance—it came so much nearer being a prison than ever. And all to keep away the union people from taking down the girls. He thought he was smart, but us girls are just as smart, or even smarter, than he is. I made believe I wanted to work for him; told him what a good worker I was, where I was employed and a whole string of fibs why I'm out of a job just now. Mr. Levinson was delighted, took me up to the workroom and promised to employ me steadily. But when the afternoon whistle blew for the girls to get back to their machines the most of them had come down with me, not to return until the union is recognized.

As I expected, the conference proved a failure—we're to strike on. I'm not disappointed, for I felt it all along that the bosses won't give in so easily, and why should they? There's still over two weeks to the real season. They've time to lose then. And, considering the condition the most of our girls are in, I'm not surprised that the bosses hope to starve them into submission. But they forget that it ain't easy to starve these girls; they're pretty trained hands at that job.

I felt happy over this morning's success, but the afternoon put a damper over me. We were holding a joint conference with the Levcovitch people and it goes without saying that Sam, who is such a wonderful exception to the most of our men, was the chairman. Poor devil! when we were in the heat of discussing a new scheme of dealing with the scabs we were all startled by an irritated woman's voice: "For shame on you, Sam; you're chinning here with the girls, while your poor wife is most dyin'."

Terribly frightened, Sam jumped from the chair and ran right out, leaving hat, coat, meeting and all. And no wonder—he's just married one year and didn't have time to tire of his wife. This is the reason he worries so much because he can't support her just at present, when she needs all the care and attention—the woman is to become a mother any minute.

This makes me think of the fuss some people make of their first born and I don't know as they can be blamed for doing it, but here is one coming and not a cent in the house for the most necessary things, not to say of a doctor, medicine, nurse and all such things that follow sickness. People throw up to us that we needn't strike, for we're sure to get married. Here's a girl that had worked for many a year side by side with the man she married, always for a little less than he did, with the result that she didn't help herself, but dragged him down.

Poor fool! she married him and hoped to be happy, but how could she when the shadow of starvation is always hovering over their door.

The baby was born dead; perhaps it's better for it, but the mother is very ill, and in such circumstances! Big, handsome Bill heard of it and gave me $5 for Sam. Bill's all right, he is. I've often watched his actions to his good wife Bertha, and I've come to believe they're more like two good chums than husband and wife. That's what I call worth while being married. They say Bill is a Socialist, and I must add, if all the Socialists treat their wives as good as he does it's worth while marrying a Socialist.

The five-dollar bill will come in very handy for Sam, but how long will it last? So far the young wife clung to every bit they had in the house, for the articles were mostly wedding presents, but now I can see Sam taking them one by one to the uncle who prospers on the people's misfortunes. I know Sam; he's the kind that would rather die than go back on his fellow-workers. He'll just keep on fighting and believing as long as there's life in him. But why should this world be divided up so unevenly—so much misery on the one end and too much happiness on the other? This can't be right. I say the Lord bless the Socialists, if they mean, earnestly, to change things for the better.

December 11

I can't say that I felt very comfortable when Leonora brought me up to that swell hotel. I was really upset by the wealth and beauty amid which I found myself. Why, the carpets were so thick that my feet just sank into them. And the magnificent pictures, the artistic decoration and so many, many flowers, and at this time of the year! I certainly never saw anything to beat it.

I wonder where the saying of the Bible that "God is our father and we are all kin to each other" fits in this case? How is it possible that us girls are sisters to these rich women? If we were I hardly think they'd be so rich and us so poor. It ain't likely that a father should want to make such a marked distinction between his children. And granted that it was his fancy to do it, they should, by rights, have some sisterly feeling for us. They should want to do for us as they want us to do for them. But it ain't so. They've everything of the best and the nicest, don't really know what to do with their time and money, knowing that many of us girls ain't got a bit of bread. Oh, that cry for bread! It's rising ever louder; I'm getting so that I can hear it in my sleep.

And this may account for my unwillingness to go and mingle with those rich, but Leonora said it will help the girls greatly, so I went. We were brought into an immensely large room with a beautiful floor that made me feel like getting hold of somebody and have a turn or two. But what struck me most was that the several women, old and young, were dressed like spring chickens. And the way they directed their opera glasses at us! as if we were a show all by ourselves.

Leonora was introduced first, and as she started to talk the tears commenced to roll from her eyes. I've often wondered where she gets so many of them. But they didn't prevent her from telling the women in her own taking way the sad story of the shirt made by her mother and grandmother in Ireland and by herself in New York. A story of work, suffering, privation and self denial; a story of love for kin as strong as death; of the unknown virtues of the poor that, if they were disclosed, would astound the world even more than their so much talked of vices. The women listened intently to every word she said; they sat there as if rooted to the floor, and what wonder! I in their place would have felt like two cents. They should have been ashamed of wearing all those diamonds and velvets and laces. But somehow I failed to see it.

When Leonora stopped little Clara rose and I felt mighty proud of that simple Jew girl. She told them point blank that she came there to ask for help, but added that it wasn't for us present, only for the thousands of young girls who've been working since they were big enough to turn a wheel, that these very hard working girls were compelled to throw up their jobs, for they couldn't go on any longer; that they're down and out at present and that there ain't a bit of fire in their grates nor a piece of bread in their cupboards, while they are out on the streets fighting for dear life. And so she said for dear life, and so they are fighting for dear life, for going back under the former conditions is worse than death.

When Clara was through I saw the handkerchiefs go up to the eyes and heard a sniffle all over the room. But here I was introduced and had to make my spiel. I don't really know how I did it; this was my first experience. But I was so excited that I just rattled off a whole lot of things. I told them that we were abused and beaten and sent to prison for no worse crime than the desire to earn an honest living; that us girls are just being pushed and tempted to take up a life of shame, and asked them if they found themselves in place of us girls if they were hungry and tired and just beaten and hounded for wanting to be honest, whether they wouldn't turn the other road, if only for spite?

They felt so terribly sorry for us that each one of them gave from $5 to $10, but what's that to them? As much as if I'd given a nickel or even less. And now they're back again among their swell society, having a good time—I even doubt whether they'll give a second thought to all the things we've told them about.

December 12

Had quite a scrap with pa early in the morning and later another with Jim. Pa wanted to know whether I've made up my mind to listen to the advice of sensible people or was still determined to follow that motley crowd of mad women, saying that the women in general have gone stark mad nowadays.

But what got me huffy was his declaration that it was silly to make so much fuss over a bunch of foreigners, when the proper thing to do was to ship them back where they came from instead of letting them prey upon our free land. Well, I must admit that I told pa a thing or two, more than ma, or Sis would ever dare to say to him. And I don't care about it, either. I won't stand for anybody insulting my friends, father or no father. And the idiocy of it all! Here are thousands of young girls who have come to this country strong and full of desire to do things, but after slaving for a few years in the land of the free they have neither health nor money; they've become poorer and our country richer. It stands to reason that our generous country is robbing them instead of being robbed.

Pa, he was just wild at me, while Ma and Sis looked as if they thought I had gone mad. Talk about Sunday being a day of rest! Not for me; it seems there's no rest for us girls nowadays. To tell the truth, I've come to wish there wasn't such a thing as Sunday. For me, at least, it only means additional aggravation.

What my family fears most is that I may cause them to die of shame on the day of my disgrace, the nature of which I really don't know myself and I'm wondering if it shall be a great or little thing. But I and all the souls in pain who fight for a decent life right here, we can't really stop to think whether we are doing a great or little deed.

It goes without saying that I didn't go to dinner with the rest, and as soon as Jim showed up went out. I was glad to go anywhere, only to be away from home.

Some one at home must have hinted to Jim about what took place in the morning, for he looked wistfully at me as soon as we were alone and muttered between his teeth, "Curse it!"

"Why, Jim, what are you cursing about, and on Sunday at that?" "I'm cursing that blame strike of yourn," says he. "Before that nuisance took place you were perfectly satisfied with your lot, obeyed your father and cared and believed in me as every good woman should do, and now you seem so changed that I often wonder what has come over you."

"Why, Jim, my boy," I said, quietly. "I've grown up since then and learned a thing or two. A tin rattle and a funny man can't satisfy me any longer. I've come to understand that, until I left the work-bench on that Tuesday morning, I had lived in a trance without really knowing why I kept it up from day to day. I was no better than the cow in the stall—as long as I had enough to eat I was satisfied. But I'm sure, Jim, that even you wouldn't want me to remain a cow."

"I—I don't know what I'd want; I'd want you to be a woman and not a freak," blurted out Jim at last.

"I wonder what a man means when he says he'd want you to be a woman? If to believe in everything that's right, to sorrow for the needy, to help the weak, to censure the wicked, to refuse being stepped upon, used and abused, means not being a woman, then I don't want to be a woman. Honestly, I don't. My Ma is considered a good woman—she wakes up long before sunrise and she works and works until we are all in bed. And she never has her say, but does what Pa wants her to do."

"Mary!" exclaimed Jim in anger. "I'm sure you'll rue the day you've mixed yourself up with those darn anarchists. They'll be the ruin of you," and with this he left me standing near the house and rushed off.

I know that I may never see his face in this world again, for like two doomed ships we've crossed each other's path and then rushed on, each to what we think is our goal. And my own feelings ain't the worst, either, for they'd kill me at home if they knew about this quarrel.

December 13

Lord, but it rained today—as if the heavens had opened to wash the world's sins away. The funniest winter ever—almost the middle of December and nothing but rain. In a way it is better for the poor devils; they can't freeze to death.

But the rain didn't keep us girls from crowding the Grand Central Palace. Even long before the appointed time the doors were thrown open and tramp, tramp came the heavy steps of wet feet upon the stone stairs. But, alas! it wasn't for a dance or entertainment that we went there on this gloomy day. The starved, despairing and irritated girls came together to find out what the bosses said to our committee. We were all anxious to hear what the committee had to tell us.

The latter did not keep us waiting very long; they were right there on the job and I must give credit to the people who chose them for us—they couldn't have made a better choice. I think that the little Jew lawyer has a better gift of the gab and more brains than any man I've ever come across. I wasn't that stuck on the other fellow, but then he was in good company and was sure to keep straight.

Earnestly, without any flourishes, the lawyer told us just what reply he had received in answer to his proposition to settle the matter by mutual agreement. They didn't want to make any settlement. It seems they've changed their minds about their proposition to sugar-coat the bitter pills they want us to keep swallowing. Perhaps they are afraid it may turn our heads. The lawyer said they don't want to yield one jot as far as the union is concerned. Talk about us being children of the same father, I'm sure they don't treat us like sisters!

The committeeman then said that if the bosses tell us there's nothing to arbitrate it's best for us to take them at their word—

they'll have to come and settle with us without an arbitration—just give in, that's all. He then hinted that some fake labor leader had promised the bosses to settle the whole strike over night, and, of course, favorable to them—all for a couple thousand of dollars.

I'd like to see him do it—he's mistaken if he thinks he could bunco us girls as he kept buncoing the workmen all this while. Us girls wouldn't hear of going back without the union, even if he stood on his head.

As the lawyer rightly pointed out to us, the trade is mending, the bosses have big orders on hand on which they hope to make a lot of money and as they can't do it without our help, and all we ask of them is a little bigger share of our hard-earned money, so as to be able to have a roof over our heads and stop being starved, they'll be sure to change their mind when they are hard pressed for workers.

It just makes my heart burn when I come to think that here are they that's living in palaces and spending money like dirt, but are that greedy that they refuse the bit we are asking. But as the lawyer told us, well and good, if they choose to turn us down in that manner, let them; but us girls must have our demands for all that. And it can't be otherwise—the union is now the only means of assuring our daily bread and with it our life; that's just why they fight it so hard.

"You're all right!" yelled the girls when both men stopped talking. "We stand by the union until we die!" But even as they uttered that cry I could hear the sound of suffering in their voices, which were shrill and hoarse, many of the girls being too hungry to yell naturally. As it was the union had to pay their car fares, for the most of them ain't got 10 cents to their name.

What I'm mostly surprised at is the other unions. How can they look on at our distress and keep quiet? Do they forget that this is the first real girl's strike? And the sufferers are just drooping down one after another, like withered flowers. To tell the truth, I ain't much better off except for what I eat at home; but things are becoming so disagreeable up there that I almost choke with every bite. I can already see the time when I'll stop coming home altogether. As Pa's mouthpiece, Ma does her job even better than he himself could do it. I'm peltered with words all the time I'm in the house.

December 14

Three weeks is about all I could stand of the strike. Now my little money is gone and this morning I had to ask Ma for a half dollar. I had no car fare to go downtown with. But Ma, she said she'd be blessed if she would give it to me, that it was hard for Pa to keep up this big household, and that he didn't propose to keep me on his shoulders much longer; that Sis was now big enough to get a steady and that it was high time that I got a home of my own, for I was spoiling the girl's chances.

Her string of words got me so mad that I could have cried from anger, but I wouldn't give her the satisfaction. So I put on my hat and coat and walked out into the street. My people are sorely mistaken if they think that they can compel me to drop this strike.

Once in the street I stopped right in front of the house. I couldn't go downtown, for I hadn't a cent to my name—a very unpleasant feeling, I must say, is to be penniless. But on the other hand, it made me feel the more keenly for our poor girls who are penniless most of the time.

Talk about women being schemers, I don't think there's anybody to beat us at that, and that's just why we are going to win. If I had no cash I had some little jewelry, so I made my way straight to the pawnshop. But when I got right close to it my heart went pitter patter—I couldn't enter. Finally, the knowledge that I was due downtown early gave me courage and I went in.

I've always dreaded the thought of having to resort to a pawnshop, but not until I had to deal with one to-day did I realize what it felt like to be one of its victims. God! it just cuts you to the heart to see all the things they've got in there. The tears came into my eyes at the sight of a pair of baby shoes. I couldn't help thinking of all the pain it gave the mother to give them up. It ain't easy to take the shoes off your baby's little feet and all for want of bread! I can't make it out: "Why should bread be so dear and human flesh so cheap!

As I looked upon the many wedding rings I thought of Sam and his wife. The woman wouldn't part with her wedding ring unless it was a case of life and death, and, to tell the truth, I don't think any woman would. It must have been real distress that made them do so. Where, then, were the husbands who had promised to protect and care for them when they gave them the rings?

I don't really know what came over me; all of a sudden the light went out of my eyes and instead of different articles it seemed to me that the whole place was just chock full of people's tears and people's sighs. It was like in a dream that I heard the man talk to me and offer a dollar and a half on my little ring, for which I paid five. It didn't matter, I was glad to get that much. A dollar and a half would keep me going for the rest of the week. I've learned the trick how to live on almost nothing.

Had plenty of excitement when I got down town. We thought that everything was O.K. when we decided last week that we won't go back without the recognition of the union. But I guess we forgot to reckon Mr. Hayman's activity. He spent the Sunday visiting some of our girls and promising them a golden egg from a goose that'll die even before it's hatched. He's shrewd. He knows that he can bunco some of the girls to his heart's content. But I honestly believe he's found a match in others. The thing that made me furious was the fact that Mame, her that's been a good friend to me, was the chief go-between. No wonder I licked her the other day—I must have had a premonition. Sorry I didn't make a better job of it, so she couldn't do any mischief for a while to come. We had our hands full with many and I'm almost sure there's more trouble to come. What with the increasing cold and sickness, with the ever growing persecution of the police and judges and the effect of failure of the arbitration committee, we're sure to lose bunches of girls, not to say anything of the men. It's one thing to come to a meeting and grow enthusiastic and shout and promise to hold out and quite another to come home cold and hungry and find nothing but reproach and misery, which is the lot of the most of us.

December 15

Lord! it must be pretty near morning. I'm all dazed. I'd just come back from that living hell called night court. I can just see my finish with the folks at home after this. Pa won't stand for one of his daughters being out the whole night. He has always been very strict on that point. And I'm in doubt whether any explanation will do me any good. For all I know this may be my last night at home. It ain't that I care for this place particularly. I have no reason to of late, but I've nothing better to turn to. And still and all, when worst comes to worst I'll go. I just won't stand for their abuse and insinuations.

But the night court! Will I ever forget it? I'm still haunted by the memory of my night's neighbors. I'm sure nobody could help cursing the world we're living in after spending a few hours in that place. God! it makes my blood boil when I think of the way they're treated down there. The insect under our feet is thought more of than these unfortunate women, and yet they, too, were carried under a mother's breast, rocked, cuddled and petted in a mother's arms. They, too, were once young and pure and honest like the judge who comes there night after night to sit in judgment over them. I just wondered if he had a heart in the right place. It seemed to me that any sane person could understand after looking at them and listening to some of the things they say that none chose their horrible trade of their own free will. There was always some cause for their downfall, and man was always the one to help them down the slippery road.

I won't be surprised if I can't sleep for many a night to come. Their shadows, the way they've been brought into court will always stand out before my eyes. They were either over or under dressed; some still with a chance for recovery; others too old for any remedy. A child of sixteen seduced by her employer wanted some redress, another not much older was accused of trying to rob an imaginary victim, who professed to've been lured to her room. It made me furious to see the judge accept his words like those of an honest man and shut her off without a chance to state her case. If the rascal was as honest as the judge supposed him to be, why did he go with her? I wish I could have told the two of them what I thought of their behavior. The poor kid didn't have ten cents, not to say the ten dollars she was fined, and will have to go to the workhouse.

"He's an honest man and you, too, judge, are honest," she whispered as she was being taken back to the cell. Her words made me think of those uttered by Christ: "He who is himself pure should throw the first stone at her." I doubt if that judge could have done that.

A woman pointed to the policeman on the stand and said that he had been taking her blood money for many a month, but since she had been sick and come down lower on the ladder of degradation she can't afford to pay and was brought here to be sent away, perhaps, for six months. But to whom could the outcast tell her tale of woe, who would listen to her? Hers seems worse than the leper's misery; she has none to ask for help on the day of need. Is it a wonder that they turn to drink? Who can blame them for doing so? I think they'd go mad if they didn't.

I was so taken up with these poor wretches that I never thought of myself and the other thirteen striking girls that were arrested with me. I was just all pity for the women I used to despise like so many of us do who don't know any better.

Our girls were all fined from ten to twenty-five dollars apiece. I being arrested the second time was fined twenty-five dollars and the judge warned me to keep out of his way or he'll send me to the workhouse the next time. I listened to him and said "Yes, sir," but he needn't think that I'll give up the strike on that account.

I think I hear some one moving about; won't be surprised if it is ma. She must have heard me come in. I'll just turn out the gas and make believe I'm asleep, or she is sure to start a row right now. And I need some rest; my head didn't touch the pillow as yet, and who knows if I'll have a pillow to touch tomorrow.

December 16

Just as I thought; pa stayed home this morning—to settle it all with me as he said. I never saw anybody more infuriated than he was. He just wouldn't listen to me telling him that I'd been arrested and taken to night court, where I was until I got home early this morning.

And strange as it may seem, my own father accused me and the rest of the girls of being a fickle lot. I didn't ask him to forgive me, nor did I cry, not even when he said that I was no kin of his if I'm to stay longer with the girls, and grabbed me and shook me up until I gasped for breath. But it pained just the same when he threw me down on the floor like one would a poisonous snake and ran out of the room hurling a terrible oath on my head.

But, hard as he was with me, ma's treatment was even worse. No sooner was she alone with me than she commenced the tongue lashing that hurt even more than father's blows. I did not reply; I had no word to say; it was too terrible to hear my own parents, them that have brought me into this world of their own accord, call me such terrible names and charge me with deeds that my worst enemy wouldn't dare to do. I just told ma that I didn't know who would be to blame if I should go wrong, for she never gave us girls a thought since we were big enough to be out and about. She never had time to guide us in our plays, choose our friends, or warn us against the many pitfalls that we met in our search for work and while working. Then what right did she have to wake up at this late hour and accuse me of having gone wrong? If she had taken the trouble to know something about her own children she would have been aware that I'd rather starve like a dog in the street or find consolation in the cold river than go to the bad.

I drank the bitter cup to the very bottom and half an hour later, when it was all over, I left the home of my childhood, perhaps never to return again. I couldn't say that it was easily done, but what can't be cured must be endured; my road had no turning.

Well, well, of all the miserable days that I've ever spent, this was certainly the worst. I left home hopeless, penniless and trembling at the very thought of having no roof over my head. Even at this moment, though I'm under cover, desolation and heart-ache seem to press me down, and according to my present feeling I don't suppose I'll ever be happy again.

I can't say that I ain't got any friends, even if my own kin did disown me. These noble Jew girls won't desert a friend in the hour of need, and it's thanks to that sweet little Rose, who is giving her time, her life, her soul to us girls, that I'm in this place, which, though it don't feel like home, is better than the dark street.

But it's mighty hard to sit in a cold, cheerless room, knowing that everything that was once dear to your heart is slipping through your fingers as through a sieve. I remember once at the circus I was wondering at one of the men—he held a pretty bird tight in his hands and told us to watch him, but even as we looked the bird disappeared and nobody seemed to know how it happened or where it had gone. And to-day I seem to be performing a similar trick—I, too, had a wonderful bird and kept it hidden away deep in my heart, but it's going, going, and will soon be gone never to come back. I'm almost sure that Jim will go with the rest. Jim, the man whom I loved above everybody else; Jim, who was my idol, my life, my all! But so much has happened since I felt that way that I don't seem to care any longer. It's strange how one can change so quickly, but I look at things from a different point today—it ain't Jim's comfortable living that I care for, and even his affection don't seem to attract me now that I see our thoughts and beliefs drifting further and further apart. How long could this mad passion last, and what then? To tell the truth, I'm just dreading the thought of tying myself to him forever and a day. And it will probably be for the best if we never meet again. But it ain't an easy job, this tearing of all ties; it's bound to tear something in your heart which can never be mended again. But why worry over all these things? The best thing is to set a lock upon one's thoughts and go on with one's task.

December 17

This world is certainly a funny game; a body can never tell what card will strike you next. There I was so hungry and didn't know where my next meal was to come from and here I am sitting at a heavily-laden table and feasting my eyes on food that probably costs more than Mrs. Bloom spends in a whole week for her family of five.

But, somehow, I didn't enjoy it—scarcely took a morsel of

it. Nor did Miss Morgan's presence seem to add relish to it all. On the contrary, the valuable silverware, the beautiful flowers, the wonderful music all threw a gloom over me. I couldn't help comparing it with the breakfast I had this morning in Mrs. Bloom's kitchen—seven of us, some standing, others sitting on a chair, a box or washtub, each holding a roll and a cup of weak coffee.

The very thought of it made me furious; I couldn't forgive myself for sitting at this rich board; my place was with the girls who can't even afford a bit of butter to moisten their bread earned in the sweat of their brow. And I wasn't a bit ashamed of my feeling; had they asked me I would have said it right out, for what have they done that us working people should have a liking for them?

To read the newspapers one would really think that they're doing the Lord knows what for us girls, but they ain't; our children down on the East Side keep dying like flies for want of feed and a bit of warmth; us girls are in such terrible trouble with the police and courts, but how many came to our aid? We are half starved, our thin bones shiver under the scant clothes and what does their help amount to in comparison with their incomes? No, it's the poor and the poor alone who would make a sacrifice every time for their own poor.

They've brought me to their fashionable clubhouse to hear about our misery. To tell the truth, I've no appetite to tell it to them, for I've almost come to the conclusion that the gulf between us girls and these rich ladies is too deep to be smoothed over by a few paltry dollars; the girls would probably be the better off in the long run if they did not take their money. They would the sooner realize the great contrast and the division of classes; this would teach them to stick to their own. But say and think what I please, we simply have to go to them for the present and accept as little or as much as they're willing to give. The lines down at Clinton Street are growing daily. And it ain't for curiosity that they come there and shove and push, only to get a bit nearer to the sacred door behind which sits Mr. Shindler. No, it's nothing but merciless hunger that brings them there.

The women gave us a thousand dollars, but what does this amount to? Not even a quarter apiece for each striker, and I know of many that need at least a ten-dollar bill to drive the wolf away from the door. And can there be a worse wolf than the landlord when there's two months' rent due him?

Only this morning as I was leaving home I walked past an evicted family. It almost broke my heart to see their pitiful faces. Can they be blamed for insisting that their daughters give up the strike and go back to work? Some of these people hadn't a cent to their name when the strike first started and one can imagine the state they're in after almost four weeks of idleness.

I can't understand somehow where in this world the justice comes in as it is arranged just now—here's us that work hard and steady and must face starvation as soon as we cease to work, while them that's idle have more money and good things than they really know what to do with.

I think it's foolish of us working people to accept our fate so quietly. It can't be that we are doomed to go through life in misery and darkness, without a ray of natural light in the shop, without a bit of sunshine at home. Can't the working people realize that we are at the complete mercy of selfishness and greed? I did to-day when I was brought face to face with all those riches; if they'd know what's good for them they wouldn't bring us in their midst, for, if anything will, this is sure to arouse the spirit of rebellion. I know it did in me. I felt sore for the rest of the day.

December 18

Met Jim this morning. I guess he must have been watching out for me. "Mary, I want to talk to you," said he, taking me aside. I felt a queer feeling come over me, but said nothing and followed him for a half block or so without either one of us speaking up when Jim, he says to me:

"Mary, I've heard about everything that had happened home. I can't say that I approve of your father's action, but, Mary, you have to acknowledge that you, too, were wrong. Can't you see, girl, how silly it is, to say the least, your going around with this gang? And where is the earthly use for it? Here am I, that cared for you as you were—simple, jolly, care-free and good. I don't want your high-falutin ideas; give them up and I'm ready to offer you a home and a strong protecting arm. You'll be my wife and mind my home and I will work for you and care for you; you won't have to bother about anything."

My lips trembled; the words wouldn't come to them for a while, so irritated was I at his talk—and suppose a girl does get married? Does that mean she has to be dead to everything else? To tell the truth, I was never so sure that a working girl gained so very much by getting married. I always felt that us girls do it more because we can't help ourselves. But I've been cured, so I spoke my mind: "Nay, Jim," said I; "I can't be your wife; it's all been a mistake between us."

"Not my wife!" exclaimed Jim in a shocked voice. "And can you explain the reason for it?"

"Yes, Jim," said I. And I reminded him what I told him some time ago; that I've grown up, and added that I was pretty nigh tired of being taken care of and if I ever got married I'd want to mind our home and take care of our children, or, in short, I explained to him that I'd want to be a partner to the game, and left him before he had a chance to say another word. The world keeps moving and everybody gets a chance at snubbing as well as being snubbed, and I had mine. Jim needn't think that he's everything because he happened to be born a man.

People say there ain't an ill wind but blows somebody good, and that was true of me today. I was so miserable this afternoon when I got back from my meeting with Jim that I felt as if I would be glad for somebody to dig a deep ditch and let me just sink into it. But the excitement and search warrant against Bekky made me forget some of my own troubles.

Bekky is one of our dare-devils—the judge placed her under bonds and she couldn't go near the factory so she followed the forelady of her shop across the river and laid it into her so she won't be able to sit for a long time to come.

When her boss, Goldstein, found it out he took out the warrant, and got his brother-in-law, Hirsh, to find Rebecca. The girls went wild when they saw Hirsh come into our meeting room—Hirsh, he was their pest while they were working and is something worse since the girls are out on strike.

But Rebecca, she was the first to spy him, and the minute he reached the front door she switched down the back stairs and into the kitchen, donned a big apron and sat down in a dark corner peeling potatoes. We girls nearly burst our sides laughing while the detective kept searching for her from the roof to the basement, looking into every closet, but he ain't no match for Rebecca; she knew how to evade him when he got very close to her. Hirsh and the other fellow spent there a couple of hours and went home, while Rebecca was whizzed off in an automobile as soon as it got dark. She'll stay with one of them millionaires until the danger is over. I tell you what, clothes do make a difference. Rebecca looked as nice as the best of them when she was togged out in one of those ladies' clothes, so as not to be recognized. And I wished so much that every one of us girls could dress that nice, and I don't know as anybody could blame us for wanting pretty things—we're still young and would like to appear to our best advantage.

But now that I'm home again I can't help thinking of Jim and that last scene between us. I know it's all for the best, but when I come to think how much I cared for him once upon a time it makes me miserable.

December 19

Today is Sunday, so I stayed home for a change. I went to see Minnie, poor girl; she's down with the fever. I knew there wasn't a cent in the house, so I pawned some of my last trinkets and brought her some change; made believe it's from the union or she wouldn't have taken it at all.

It just cut me to the heart to enter that basement flat—dark, musty and so low that I could hardly stand upright, and I ain't very big. Poor Minnie; she's only a shadow of her former self. She didn't know me or Ray, who came along with me. Somehow she took me for the judge, the one that had such a great share in hounding us girls, and if I hadn't darted aside she would have surely jumped at me.

I tried to induce her mother to send her to a hospital, but she wouldn't hear of it. She has still the old-fashioned idea that a hospital ain't nothing but a poorhouse. Poor, old lady, she's had her share of suffering. But this strike, which enlisted two of her daughters, the main breadwinners, was the hardest of all. And now, thanks to the brutality of the police, Minnie is down and out, and who knows if she will ever get better?

We stayed there a while, then did some picket duty and went to the Church of Ascension. And of the pleasant things that have happened to me during the past few weeks—and they were mighty few, I must say—this sermon was the best. It wasn't about religion at all, nor about heaven nor hell; just about the men and women we meet with every day of our lives, the injustices we are suffering under and the hope for a better future. His text was: "For the needy shall not always be forgotten, the expectation of the poor shall not perish forever."

The minister spoke of the army of unemployed who stand for hours in line in order to get a cup of coffee and a bit of bread, and of the unfortunate women who are compelled to barter their very flesh for a bit of bread, and of the many crimes committed for nothing but the necessity to satisfy the craving of the stomach, and of the mothers who can't get any bread for their suffering children and welcome the latter's death as a relief from suffering; of the numerous pitfalls open to the daughters of the poor. But, said he, "For all that and all that, the poor are not forgotten, their hope of coming into their own will yet be realized, for they're the masters of the world after all—it is they that are building the houses and running the railroads and baking the very bread they ain't got to eat, and lighting the streets and sailing the ships and making the clothing."

Then he turned to our strike and said that woman today is doubly a slave; that she has a twofold task to perform and it isn't her place to spend ten hours a day at the machine, and there isn't a person with a clear conscience living who wouldn't think that fifty-two hours is long enough or even too much. But, said he, "The wicked have overdrawn the lines at last, for even the weakest of the weak—woman has risen in rebellion against the terrible oppression. And as through her cometh man's life, so through her shall come his liberation."

As I sat there listening to those words of wisdom I suddenly saw myself in another world where the working people have thrown off all the fetters that have kept them bound to their bosses, and were themselves enjoying the fruit of their labor instead of feeding an army of idlers. I felt as though I was sitting in the people's church after they had come into their own and tears of joy and happiness were trickling down my face, but I minded them not; I was eager to embrace and join hands with God's children—man, woman, Jew, Gentile, dark and white alike.

On our way home we turned around the corner of Grace Church; it was all a-glittering with gold and beautiful lights, while a few steps away the bread line was rapidly forming, though it was still lacking two hours to the time of distribution. I wanted to stop there and tell those miserable, degraded men what I had just heard and the bright hope I'm cherishing for them, but I knew they weren't in the mood to listen to words. They wanted bread.

December 20

Lord! I do wish they'd stop to muddle us girls with their attempts of settlement. I'm pretty sure it's all her, that sleek temptress. The serpent that tempted Eve was cursed by the Lord: "Because thou hast done this thou art cursed above all cattle, and above every beast of the field; upon thy belly shalt thou crawl and dust shall thou eat all the days of thy life."

I'm inclined to believe that these curses ain't strong enough for her that's mixing in our affairs. I've come to realize that there ain't no worse plague than a false labor leader. For the best of them ain't nothing but a crouching, miserable instrument of the bosses. The latter have at least the courage to come right out with the goods. They don't hesitate to say that they ain't got any love for the working people. But this ain't the case with the other leeches; they twine around our bodies, holding us down tight, while they themselves yield their head and extend their necks to the bosses.

It makes me wild to see that woman in our midst. And I'm almost sure that we ain't going to succeed until we make an effort to shake off these serpents. I think we ought, by rights, forbid these hirelings to trample upon us. It's my honest opinion that us girls ought to be allowed to manage our own affairs and I told her so, too. Came pretty near having a real fight with her. She ain't satisfied with arranging all these tom-fool conferences—nay, she must needs give out false reports to the newspapers. I wonder who gave her the authority to do so? I'm sure it ain't the League women, for they ain't got much love for her neither. But she's mistaken if she thinks she can fool us girls into submission by any of her tricks.

What gets me is the idea of some people that us working girls don't know nothing. Beginning with our bosses, who would go wild if we dared tell them that we're every bit as good as their own women folks, and ending with those leeches of ours? But when we come to think of it, us girls are every bit as good or even better than them, for they never turn their hands into a bit of useful work, while us girls help share the world's burdens all the time.

To tell the truth, I often wonder where the justice comes in in this world of ours—here's us that work hard and ain't got nothing, while those that's idle get all the fat plums and boss us about into the bargain.

But this doesn't mean that we're to be left all by ourselves in this terrible fight. I don't see why the other unions don't take a hand in it. Us girls have relied upon our own strength as long as we could bear it. But we've at last come to a pass where it's impossible to go on that way much longer. We simply must get assistance somewhere.

Went up to the teamsters this evening. I guess there is some unknown tie between us working people, only we didn't come to understand it as yet. I felt perfectly at home when I found myself in the midst of these grim, rough-looking men. And the reception they gave me was so different from the one we received from the rich ladies. Here you could feel that you've met with a kindred spirit. When I saw the hardened, gray-haired old men cry like children at our tale of woe, I got more confidence in our struggle, for I knew that we won't be allowed to starve to death as long as there's such sentiments expressed for us.

"Brothers," said their president when I was through talking, "I needn't say that us working people have a feeling of admiration for these brave girls." And he went on describing our devotion to the cause and telling them so many, many things which made my ears burn. But I was all attention when he got to the point that it ain't only our struggle that us girls are fighting, but the battle of the entire working class, for woman's demand for equal wages with men will put a stop to the bosses discharging men workers whenever they can and supplanting them with women. I thought that this plain driver had hit the nail right on the head. In his own simple way he had thought it all out. And a new hope arose in my sore heart—that the working people are sure to reason out their condition before long and as soon as they do they're bound to find the right way out of it. The hard-working boys had no money in the treasury, so they taxed themselves a half a dollar each and gave me $24 and said to come again when we need more.

December 21

It did my heart good to see the little girls come back from the workhouse. The bosses and their barkers, the judges, needn't think now that they can break our strike by sending some of us to prison. I must say it must be a sad disappointment to them.

I would have just loved to let them have at least one glance at little Rebecca as she landed from the ferry boat where so many of us girls were waiting for her. "Girls," she said to us, with a loud laugh, "don't worry about going to the workhouse. It ain't worse than our own factories are." When one of the reporters got to questioning her, she said: "You can say in your papers that the sending us across the river won't break the strike; nothin' doin' in that line."

"Say, Mary," she whispered to me a few minutes later, when we were away from the rest of the crowd, "my knees are sore to the bone from scrubbin' an' do you know I'm almost starved. And, say, it's enough to kill a body, the company you meet there is."

Well, well, they may talk all they want about great heroes and heroines—our girls are the real stuff. To tell the truth, I don't know as they could act different if they wanted to—the road to freedom ain't got no byways—a body must continue to march forward on a straight path or turn coward and traitor, but us girls ain't built that way.

It was real touching to see that old Italian whose daughter had been to the workhouse with the other girls. At first, when he heard of what he called her disgrace, he cried and lamented. The poor simpleton thought he's sure to have an old maid on his hands now, for no man would care to marry a convict, but when he saw all the homage that was being paid to the girls, and the beautiful flowers they received, he broke down and confessed it was wrong of him to stand in her way and he wouldn't care if she stays out as long as it will be necessary.

I wish we'd have many Italian fathers like him, for we have our hands full with them. I don't really know what we would do if it wasn't for the Italian Socialists. The Italian girls are like a lot of wild ducks let loose. I ain't a bit surprised that our bosses are so anxious to replace us girls by Italians—they're good workers and bad thinkers—just what suits the bosses, but it is pretty hard on us. To tell the truth, I don't know as these simple souls can be blamed much—their thinking machines were never set in working order.

I think that of all the people I know the Italians treat their women the worst—they grow old before they've a chance to be young. What a world of difference between them and the Jew girls.

But I think there'll be some change all around. The plain, rough driver told the truth—this first girls' strike is a fight for the future of the millions of people to follow us. If we only had many men like him! I've often asked myself what keeps the men from doing something for us women and have pretty nigh come to the conclusion that it's their foolish desire to be it. I guess they're afraid that us women will outdo them when we get down to do things in a business-like way.

They're quick enough, though, to raise a row if us women would go scabbing on them. But it's really their turn now on the scabbing line. We've had our hands full this afternoon with a gang of men who couldn't be persuaded to join the union when it took only a few minutes to get every one of the girls in that workroom to become members.

I was mighty glad for the plain talk some of the girls gave them. "If you ain't going with us now, then you're against us," said Pauline, and with this she jumped to the door, opened it wide and exclaimed: "Go, or we'll make hash out of you before very long." And I tell you what, it worked like magic—the cowards feared the girls' strength and after some more grumbling and protesting had finally paid in a few cents each and gave in their names. "Don't fret," said Clara to me later, "we're going to make them plunk up the rest. There are more of us in the workroom than their kind and they ain't nothing but trash, anyway." Honestly, my head goes round and round from the many things we see and have to go through, but it's all right.

December 22

Lord, what a miserable night I spent! The girls told me that Jim was around looking for me and I felt sorry for the chap, and, another thing, Clara handed me a note and made me promise to keep it sealed until this morning. At daybreak I couldn't wait any longer and tore the envelope—I can't really say what I felt then—it said that by the time I'd open this note she'd be dead and free from suffering. Poor, poor, girl! She's lost all her strength in fighting her way through, one may say, since she was big enough to walk about. It seems to me that she feared she'd weaken and give in to the enemy, so rather than do that she made an end of it all. But it's just like her to think of us girls, even while she was about to die; her last words were for me.

For a brief moment I was like thunderstruck; the next I fetched my hat and coat and started for Brooklyn, where Sarah was boarding. Even to the last minute I had a faint hope that she may be alive and I'd save her from self-destruction. She was still warm when we got into her room and took off the noose from her neck; her face was scarcely whiter than the night before, when she gave me that fatal note, but her head fell lifeless on our hands when we tried to put her down on the narrow cot. Her wide-open eyes stared into the unknown, her wish was fulfilled, she was free from suffering.

Stupefied, I stood gazing at her and thinking of her brief life. Did she ever live? For one can scarcely call living this miserable existence from day to day, which us working girls are doomed to, this steady sewing of sleeves, sleeves, sleeves, until the whole future presents but one monster sleeve. Sarah had made thousands upon thousands of them, and at the end of six years' work she had to take her life, for she had nothing to live upon as soon as she was out of work. She was too proud to go begging or borrowing, and was compelled to dash her ship of life to pieces.

It's terrible when we come to think that this happened here in our own free land, next door, you might say, to all these many millionaires. The working man ain't much better off than the slave, but it's worse for us girls. When the man is down and out he can still go into a saloon and get a bite to eat at a free lunch counter. He can go in and warm up his cold, shivering body, but for us there ain't nothing left but starvation or the street. If we come to reason out things Sarah can't really be blamed much for her act.

And still and all, her death broke me up for good. If she had gone wrong the judge would have sent her to prison for a few days. If she hadn't died in the attempt to do so he would have given her a year. But what else could an underpaid, overworked body do? Poor kid! There ain't even a kin of hers around to shed a tear over her corpse.

And it ain't only us waistmakers that suffer so badly, either. I went up to a meeting of the white goods makers and when I heard their troubles I thought that we ain't in it.

And there are the human hair goods makers; they, too, are striking, but to tell the truth, it seems to me that when us girls have reached a point where we understand enough to go out on strike there's still some hope for us. Take the paper box makers—they're so deep down in the mud that they can't even lift their head any longer—it's for their kind that I don't see any hope at all. Nor for the kind of people like Jim that won't simply listen to reason, just like a stubborn mule. I've cared too much for Jim not to feel bad about this parting; it tears my heart to pieces, for his sake as well as mine; I've something bigger to help me out, to make this personal sorrow insignificant, but he ain't got nothing but his own little self to think of, for he thinks of me as a part of himself; his is what I call the selfish love. I've heard women say to treat a man like a dog and he's sure to lick your fingers. If that be true Jim'll come back to me; he'll learn to love me not only for what I look, but also for what's in me, and if that should happen— well, what's the use of hoping; I've almost given it up for a bad job.

December 23

Have had a busy day and evening helping the Socialist women with the reception which they had arranged for us girls. I honestly believe that they couldn't have done anything better with their money—a body gets a few cents, buys bread and relishes it, but in a few minutes it's all forgotten and one is as blue and miserable as ever, but when one spends an evening in a brightly lit hall in company of congenial people, a good floor and some music to help glide along, I tell you what, it acts better on one's spirit than any amount of medicine. And why should it be a shame to dance, even if we are out on strike for the last six weeks, are almost starved and don't know what we'll do for food next.

If it wasn't for Sarah's death, which put a damper on us all, we would have had a real fine time. But Sarah's death came too near home and we all couldn't help thinking who's to follow. But no sooner did we bury the poor soul than we had to go back to the strike and its numerous duties, and the Lord knows they were plentiful. We can't devote much time to anything but the strike nowadays.

This is just why the dance was needed, though some people did object to it, as if us poor devils ain't entitled to a bit of fun any longer. I think I can find an excuse for those others—they had never been in our boots and don't really know what to make of us working girls. It must seem to them that we are made of different material or they wouldn't talk that way. Look at the rich kids—they attend gymnasiums and basketball and lawn tennis and tea parties and so many, many different things and everybody takes it for granted that they need it all. While it's but a few who realize that beyond the gray covers of our daily drudgery there is still hid the joy of living. That we from the East Side tenements need recreation as much as them that live in the palaces.

Had some fun! Inez gave us her car for shopping purposes, but we didn't know enough to find out whether the man who ran the car would wait for us. Rushed upstairs and got all our packages and ordered them taken to our automobile. But, Lord have mercy upon us poor souls! When we reached the street loaded with parcels like the devil with sins, there was no automobile in sight. It didn't matter so much after all—we had a good laugh at our own expense and carted the things to the hall.

When I got there Jim was waiting for me, and, by the way he acted, I'm beginning to believe he has changed his opinion about us girls. I tried to be as jolly as I possibly could under the circumstances—I don't believe of sniffling before anybody, especially Jim—I wasn't going to show him how bad I felt. What's the use? And yet, I'd be more than happy if I could turn him to my way of looking upon life. Not that I'd want to boss over him. I wouldn't want that for anything in the world—no more than I'd want him to boss over me.

The place was just jammed and Leonora had a hard job getting to the platform—she had to introduce the workhouse girls, and I must say this for her—she certainly did it in a most touching way. I perfectly agree with her that this disgraceful treatment of us girls is going to be an everlasting shame upon the heads of those cruel judges.

The girls are to get medals for bravery—it's no more than just that they should. I'm inclined to believe that they're as brave as our Revolutionary fathers themselves.

I had a few turns with Jim, but could not do much talking. He said that pa was somewhat sorry for all that happened. And a good thing that he is. For my part he can stay that way, too, but it may help the others a bit; he'll be more careful in his treatment of Sis. I wonder if she's got that steady yet which I prevented her from getting.

People say that it's an ill wind that blows nobody any good, and that is true about Sis—my sad experience will give her a chance to sponge upon pa for everything she'll want.

Poor Sarah! Perhaps if she had waited until tonight and diverted her thoughts a bit it might never have happened, but, then, who knows; perhaps she is better off after all.

December 24

It just struck me this morning that this is the second month since we are out on strike. It seems easy to say the second month. But Lord! Thirty-two whole days, 7248 hours since Clara said to us girls down at that big meeting: "Come, girls, let's go out on strike." And all those hours were hours of suffering, agony and growth. Yes, growth—whatever else we'll gain from this strike it certainly was an eye-opener to some of us, myself especially.

Only last night I spoke to Jim about my family and today I came pretty near breaking with them for good—until death would unite us once more. Had escaped arrest by a miracle. Arrest now means the workhouse—well, what of it? All my father could do is to disown me as his daughter officially. I'm most beginning to think that blood ties ain't everything after all. There's my own sister, Sis. We were nursed by the same mother, brought up under the same roof, and yet we've absolutely nothing in common.

While I was at home and as giddy as she herself we used to scrap at every opportunity. Since I grew up and became interested in other things we scarcely spoke to each other. But here's little Ray—no blood relation of mine—of a different religion, from another land, and still and all I'm sure she's more to me than any sister could be.

I've become a philosopher of late. It seems to me that this world of ours will be a better place to live in when people grow less selfish, stop thinking only of themselves and their flesh and blood and share their affections with all good people, tie or no tie.

I think that the strike has helped us girls considerably in that line. There's that feeling of kinship among us that amazes even me at times—we feel with and suffer for one another. I was so happy this morning when I noticed the girls are a bit brighter after yesterday's affair, but there were only about two thousand at the dance. The other four thousand who are still out with us felt too miserable to come.

This strike is the toughest proposition I've come across in my life. One would never believe that us girls will be able to stand all those terrible hardships. If only the union was able to give us at least a half dollar per day so as to keep the body and soul together. But this would mean three thousand dollars daily, not counting all the fines paid into court and many other expenses.

And yet, when I come to think that in this big city alone there are 55,000 union men it don't seem such an impossibility to keep us girls supplied with bread until we win. If they'd only be as thoughtful as the teamsters and give half a dollar per head it would already mean over $75,000, or in other words victory for us girls.

I've had the settled shops thrown up to me. What can we expect from them when they don't even make much now; besides, girls are girls after all and still have a great deal to learn before they will know what solidarity means.

Was sent to one of the biggest and richest unions in town this evening. The men wore their prosperity on their coat sleeves and they acted like real swells; they met behind closed doors, have a private office where committees can wait all they want until it suits the royal assembly to receive them. While I was waiting one of the men told me that their local has four hundred members, that their initiation fee is $75 and that the dues are $1.50 per month. He then added that the wages they receive are so high that there's scarcely a man among them but that's got a home of his own.

After an hour's waiting I was allowed to enter. It took a committee of three to escort me to the platform. The members were all dressed up and looked slick for fair. I thought that here I was sure to get a heavy lump for our girls and talked to the men for over twenty minutes, telling them incidents of the strike that could have made a stone shed tears. But not these people; they sat there like they were chiseled out of ice. Another committee of three escorted me out of the meeting room and a third committee informed me an hour later that they would send $25 some time soon.

December 25

The loud ringing of church bells this morning was the first reminder of Christmas—the holiday I used to await with

148

so much anticipation. The bells were telling us of peace on earth and good will toward men, but when I thought of the peace us girls are enjoying it made me smile at it all.

Don't know why, but somehow I had no heart to go to church and went picketing instead. Just as I was leaving the hall who should I meet but Jim. Poor boy! He didn't look as if he had peace, either. Something seemed to bother him. We walked along for awhile, when he said quietly: "Mary, I'd like to buy you something for the holiday, but dared not." I tell you what, Jim is mighty careful the way he treats me nowadays. He has finally learned that I, too, have to be consulted about some things. And right he was not to buy it without asking, for I wouldn't hear of it. The idea of me getting presents when the girls ain't got no bread.

Jim understood what I meant and said he'd give it to the union, then. It's all good and well for the rich to follow that custom of present giving, but why should us poor people insist upon imitating them I can't see for the life of me. We should know better than spend our hard-earned money on useless trumpery.

Jim came along with me and stood out in the cold until my time was up and another bunch of girls took our places. I'm around the Bijou nowadays. Wouldn't dare come near Haymans—I'm a marked chicken in that neighborhood. So I just exchanged places with another girl who's done her job at the Bijou until it got too hot for her to be there.

From there Jim and I walked up Fourteenth street and went into the Salvation Army headquarters to see for ourselves how people came to beg for a dinner. Lord, the most pitiful sight ever! Can there be anything worse than to see a human being full grown and healthy stretch out his hand for charity, standing in line for hours in order to get a bit of meat and a piece of bread? And what different types—some ashamed to lift their eyes, others hardened to all shame and humiliation, but all hungry and anxious to get a taste of real food, which they probably get only this once a year. I was really surprised to see the effect this had on Jim. As I looked at him it struck me for the first time that Jim was what he had been because he knew no better, because he didn't take the trouble to see all sides of life. That his heart was as good and noble as I once thought it to be, but it was covered over with a thick mass, which it was now beginning to shed.

Dear boy, his eyes filled with tears when he spied that little kid dressed in a man's worn coat and torn shoes without stockings. I'm sure she ain't more than ten years old, but the way she pushed herself to the front and looked wistfully at the spread out parcels one would have reckoned her to be an old grandmother. "The kiddies will have a fine dinner," she whispered to herself when she passed us, her arms loaded with food.

"Darn it!" exclaimed Jim, following her with his eyes. "There's surely something wrong somewhere, if a child of that age has to go begging for the kiddies, while she's scarcely more than a kid herself."

Silently, for the first time in this holy morning, I delivered a prayer to the Lord. The Jim I disliked was slipping away and a new one, nobler and more generous, was entering into my life.

We left the barracks after a while, had a bite and, I leading the way, started up Fifth avenue. I thought it was a good policy to let him note the difference. And, sure enough, he did.

"Mary," says he, "it seems to be a shame that these people gorge themselves with all good stuff, while most of the others have to stand in line in order to get their leavings. I—I really think you're about right in trying to help make things as they should be, for it seems a grievous sin to live amid all the misery without lifting a finger to help."

And so I've succeeded in awakening another human heart. I know Jim, and am sure that he won't shrink from the trials he is sure to meet on this new path of life.

December 26

Elsie and I went to a rich lawyer's house this afternoon, and upon my word, even now in winter, the place he lives in seemed wonderful to me. I can just imagine what it looks like in summer.

As I was walking up the pretty avenue and looking at the heavily curtained windows I was just thinking of the people that live behind them and wondering if they ever knew what suffering and sorrow meant. Somehow it seemed impossible to associate these two together.

I felt a bit uncomfortable when I found myself in that magnificent library, under the shrewd, scrutinizing gaze of our host. The grand dame gave me two of her bejeweled fingers and looked as if she had bestowed a great honor upon me. Their cub of a son tried to start up a flirtation, but had to give it up as a bad job. And their daughter—the only pleasing person in the room—a young sweet girl of sixteen, was glowing and looked as pretty as a rosebud.

I'm sure I ain't greedy and don't begrudge her what she's entitled to, but I couldn't help grumbling at her happy lot when compared with some of our girls. While we were waiting for the invited guests to arrive the lawyer took time to explain to Elsie that it's only the women who took up the strike and strikers as a vogue. "You'd be surprised," said he, "how much opposition this tomfoolery meets with among the men."

That's just what I thought myself, though I ain't no big or even little lawyer. But I couldn't help laughing the way Elsie gave him tit for tat. I don't really blame him for taking a liking to her—one can't help doing it. When he wanted to know why us girls stick to the union she told him that he would, too, if he had to work, for the union was the surest means of obtaining a living wage.

Then he was curious to find out who our leaders were and she replied that every other girl with brains in her head tried to lead her timid sister out of the terrible suffering they were both undergoing. When asked why us girls didn't strike before this, Elsie replied that we just woke up from a long sleep.

One of the lady visitors wanted to know why us girls don't take positions as servants if we have to live under such hard conditions while working in the factory. Her question made me that mad that for a minute I forgot where I was and said to her: "No, thanks; none of that for mine. I can't see where the improvement comes in by washing your dirty linen. If you people don't see anything better in store for us you'd better give up the idea of helping us out of our trouble."

I honestly believe it's a sin against ourselves that we are committing by going to them and telling them the mournful tale of our hardships. I'm sick to my neck of their few paltry dollars. What do I care for the $130 we collected there? I'm tired of charity. The sooner we demand justice as our right and not as a boon from the rich the better for us. It seems so silly, this traveling from mansion to mansion. It makes me real downhearted and I always wish I hadn't come.

I'm sorry this time, too. I'd much rather have spent the afternoon with Jim. I know he didn't like to see me go; he just dotes on every word I say as if I was a prophet. He realizes how much more I had learned during these weeks and ain't ashamed to learn, even if it is from a woman.

Dear Jim, I know he frets over my shabby clothes and surmises that I ain't got too much to eat. But he admires my devotion to the girls and cares more for me than he would for some of these rich ladies who come sailing among us girls and trying to pry into our very soul.

I can't help thinking of the change in his behavior toward me—it's more gentle and loving than ever, but there's a sort of dignity in it which lifts me at once to his height, which carries with it a recognition of me as a human being. I'm sure Jim is a woman's rights man, though he don't know it and probably would resent it if he did.

I'm wondering what'll happen tomorrow. I hear it rumored that we're about to be sold out. I'd like to see any one trying to sell me or any of the other girls. Not on your life! We ain't the men—us girls are on our guard against these fakers.

December 27

Early in the morning had to go to a conference of shop delegates at Beethoven Hall. As soon as I spied the shiny, smooth-chinned leader I was on my guard—knew that there was something in the air. If I had my way, say, I wouldn't trust that man with five cents, not to say with the welfare of us girls.

In his soft, snake-like voice he tried to impress upon us the necessity of coming to some understanding with our bosses, whom he had met the previous evening. It seems to me that he meets those fellows entirely too often. I tell you what, when a leader comes to you and sings a song of praise for your boss rest assured that he ain't no friend of the working people.

I let him talk to his heart's content, then asked quietly, "And what about the union? You told us all about the goodness of our bosses and nothing at all about the union."

"Now, see here," said the cur, sternly, "don't get excited and excite others with you. We'll do the best we can under the circumstances."

I felt a bit uneasy—his answer boded no good. But even then I knew it in my bones that the girls won't listen to him or his propositions unless the recognition of the union went with it. Us girls ain't going to be buncoed by those trimmers that speak and scheme to suit their own purpose. For further assurance of my convictions I looked around me, and if our fake benefactors had known the girls the way I know them I'm pretty sure they would have left out some of their hot air.

In the afternoon there were five mass meetings held in different halls in order to give all the girls a chance to vote on the latest proposition. I made it my business to have a peep at all of them, and I must say it was the greatest sight I've met yet. Girls with sore throats and girls with broken noses; girls with wet, torn shoes and girls without hats or coats, shivering from cold and faint from hunger; they were all on hand; their condition didn't matter a bit. Their vote was wanted and they came. Tired, half starved and almost dropping from weakness, they stood up on the tables, clung to the banisters, steadied themselves on window sills and hung onto the balcony railings. Their deep, thoughtful eyes wide open, their lips parted, they tried not to miss a single word uttered from the platform and the expression of their worn faces was even more eloquent than words.

Like a numberless army of bees they rose in a body against those who were trying to mar their future. "We're sick of all these assurances," shouted Fanny. "This is the time to strike them while the iron is red hot and we're going to get what we want or die in the attempt."

To listen to the numerous individual expressions one would have thought that us girls must be positive of a near victory, and yet this very morning many of the girls deserted our ranks and went back to work, but it doesn't seem to matter; somehow we've become so desperate that we look upon the whole thing this way: We don't die twice and don't live on forever, and us girls are resigned to accept whatever comes along. At any rate, it's better to die fighting than being fought with your hands tied behind your back.

"We ain't going back!" yelled Molly, jumping from a nearby table onto the platform. "I move that we remain out unless the bosses sign an agreement with the union." I'm happy to say her motion was accepted unanimously.

Could Sis ever be stirred by emotions like those that stirred my heart at that moment? Could there be a greater happiness than the happiness of living and doing for others?

As I was coming into the League after the meeting I met the silent labor leader and asked if the American Federation would be a party to the large mass meeting to be held at Carnegie Hall next Sunday.

"I don't very well see how we can do it," was his reply. I could have spit in his face for this answer, and from a representative of our mother organization! I guess he's looking out for some fat job and is afraid to displease the politicians.

I often wonder how our League women don't see through all these men. It seems strange that they should meet them on brotherly terms. I know I wouldn't want to be that man's sister!

December 28

Spent this morning in the office of the union and, honestly, it pretty near did me up—the lines of applicants for strike benefits grow hourly; as it is they already extend from the fourth 'way down to the ground floor, standing four abreast. It's enough to break one's heart to witness their misery, even for a little while. People are dying with hunger, and this, coupled with the horrible brutalities practiced upon our girls, reaches a point where description becomes impossible.

We in the office had to listen to their tales of unbearable cold, of starvation and sickness that reigns in their gloomy homes. The truth of their words could easily be verified by the care-worn expression of their pale faces. God! where do we get the power to stand it all? I myself often go for days with just a bit of dry bread, but somehow a body's insides get so dried up that one don't mind it any longer—only that our strength is giving out bit by bit.

In the afternoon I met with a lot of rich guys—representatives from different organizations, who have at last woke up and want to call a protest meeting against the outrages of the police. Lord! with whom didn't I elbow there—the boss of those who talk votes for women and those who seem to worry so much about the salesgirls and so many, many other big guys that a plain little shop girl had no show at all among them.

To-day, more than ever, it was made clear to me that money does all the talking. It was simply ridiculous to see them bow to her who owns so many millions, all except one little Jew girl and myself. It makes me laugh when I think of the woman who was so terribly excited when Miss Morgan offered her her hand. "I—I really can't, Miss Morgan; my hand is not clean," muttered the silly fool, while only a minute previous to that she shook hands with a number of ordinary mortals. But she needs polish it off before it can touch Miss Morgan's sacred flesh. And she a well known college woman!

It was funny to watch them when the question of speakers was taken up for discussion. "We don't want any agitators," protested one of the lady bosses. "We are here to see that the Carnegie meeting has the tone of respectability attached to it."

It goes without saying she means the Socialists. I couldn't help wondering why the rich are so afraid of them. Is it because the Socialists don't mince words and show them up at every opportunity?

I must say this wasn't the case at this conference. Not one of those big people present thought of treating the matter openly; on the contrary, they tried their best to arrange matters so that things should be smoothed over—a sort of mutual admiration meeting they proposed it to be.

It's sickening, and that is all there is to it; their cowardly way of doing things; always afraid of offending some one of their kind. Throwing dust into our eyes, that's what I call their conference and professed desire to take our part.

I just sat there and had a good look at those women whom we admire so much from the newspaper stories. One of the richest looked like she was used to many a spree. The other reminded me of a big, strong horse; the third was so rigged out that a body couldn't make out whether she was a person or a

mummy. And the few men present—there was no backbone
to them except one or two. I didn't feel a bit that they were
my superiors.

It seems that the morning and afternoon weren't enough for
my wrought-up nerves. When I got home I found that Mrs.
Bloom was served with a dispossess. What am I to do? Here I
am living under her roof and sharing her crust of bread whenever she's got it, without being able to repay her for the kindness. I ain't got anything for the uncle any longer and as much
as I hate the very idea of it I think I'll have to ask for strike
benefits after all. The Lord knows it ain't easy for me. I kept
from doing it for pretty nigh eight weeks, and so did most of
the other girls. But want is apt to make you do anything. People sell their honor and flesh all on account of it. Must go in
and tell Mrs. Bloom not to worry.

December 29

This was a busy day for fair! I must admit it ain't easy
sailing, the life of a newsy. We see them running about
the streets shivering from cold and perhaps from hunger, and
never pay any more attention to them than to a stray dog or cat.

It's only when a body gets right on the job, like I did today,
that one realizes what terrible hardships these small boys have
to endure. I'm still numb from cold—was out on the streets
since early in the morning until night and, as luck would have
it, this was the coldest day this winter.

People say a friend in need is a friend indeed. And the New
York Call proved to be the only true friend among all the newspapers of this large city. Its management gave us a special issue
free of charge and us girls sold it for our strike benefit. We did
it without a momentary hesitation, without a thought of the
humiliation it carried with it or the bitter cold we'd have to
endure. Us girls have gone through so many trials that it makes

no difference what we're to do so long as it is for the good of the cause. But I sometimes wonder what other experiences there are in store for us.

I've heard people call the newspapers the mouthpiece of the people. Well, I'm pretty sure that The Call is the mouthpiece of the working people, but the latter can't somehow see it.

It's funny when I think of the way many took our going out on the streets—big white sashes across our shoulders and heavy bundles of papers under the arms.

"What sort of a wrinkle is this?" muttered a well-dressed man whom I asked to buy a paper. "I think you women are going mad for fair," he added, looking at me with disdain. "Go home; woman's place is in the home."

I wonder if the man knew I had no home to go to, nor did the most of us girls who were out on the streets selling the papers.

"Won't you buy a paper?" I next asked of a woman on her way to work.

"I don't believe in this business," she replied haughtily. "There ain't no earthly use in making all that fuss when a body might just as well go to work without striking. Decent women leave that job to the men."

I watched that woman for a moment as she rushed on and pitied her for her great ignorance of her own condition.

"Can I sell you a newspaper for the benefit of the girls?" I inquired of an elderly gentleman, probably on his way to the office. He stopped and gave me one of those nasty smiles that send a chill through one's body.

"The girls," repeated the old scallawag. "Why, they have always had my admiration, but why buy the paper? I'm ready to give them money just for their good looks."

I caught his last words as I was turning the corner a few feet away from him. I was on one of the poorest spots, near Twenty-third street, and, finding that my attempt to do business there was useless, I slowly made my way down town, and the further

I went the easier it became to dispose of my load. Here the restaurant keepers allowed me to enter, warm up a bit and sell my papers, while in the swell places I was not permitted to enter the vestibule.

Down on Third street I met a poorly dressed woman, I suppose, on her way to the grocery store. She stopped, asked me for a paper and gave me a dime. "Keep the change," she said to me. "You girls need every cent you can get. My people will do without the quart of apples I was about to buy."

I took the coin from her and, on the impulse of the moment, raised it to my lips. It meant more to me than all the dollars received from the rich—hers was the true Christian spirit.

And so is that of our dear, brave girls. Half frozen and hungry, they refused to drink the hot coffee prepared for them at the headquarters of the League; they still resent every attempt of charity. And yet the coffee was bought on money they took in from the sale of papers. Why, some of us girls received as much as five dollars for a single paper. Oh, Lord! how my bones do ache and the chilblains—they're almost killing me; I could scratch off the very skin from my body. I tell you what, us girls can't be accused of weakness of character.

December 30

Well, another day spent on the streets of New York! A day of study and many experiences. I tell you what, the street is a mighty good thing if a body watches it with open eyes. I doubt if anybody could get as much out of a year's schooling as I did of the few hours of my newspaper trade.

Paid a visit down to Wall street this morning. I was somewhat anxious to see for myself what them big fellers think of our strike and us girls. But I ain't ashamed to admit that I was left in the soup—the real thing is hid behind locked doors; it's only them $10 and $20 per week millionaires that I've met, and they are the worst ever.

The way they look upon you, as if you ain't worth to tread upon God's earth, and yet, when I come to think of it, I realize that they're tradeless know-nothings who are lost as soon as they lose their job. I was so disgusted that I didn't take the trouble to say anything to them—what's the use? They don't care a rap about us girls, except in the way that old fogy did.

I felt a sinking sensation, though, when I got to Park Row. Here it was even worse. This was the first time that I came face to face with the real Bowery tramp. With bleared, bloodshot eyes, red noses, trembling hands, stooped backs and tattered clothes, they huddled together in the doorways. It was impossible for me to remain there more than a minute—this was too much for my tired nerves.

It was too painful to think that in a rich city like ours there should still exist the possibility of encountering a similar sight. I couldn't make myself believe that all these men have fallen that low of their own accord—the bread of charity can't taste good to anybody. Who, then, was responsible for their degradation?

I couldn't reflect upon the subject very long—had to get down to the Jewish theater in time for the matinee—the manager had promised to let me do business. He advised me to announce my wares from the stage and I tried to get up there. This was no easy task, by any means. Down, down I went into a dark, musty cellar, finding my way by the dim light of a small gas jet. The narrow hall was lined on both sides by two rows of small, flimsy wooden partitions.

It's hardly believable, and yet those sheds were nothing but the dressing rooms for the actors and actresses. I must say, this new discovery was a terrible shock to me. Somehow it was impossible to associate the gay men and women we meet on the theater stage with the life in a cold, dark cellar. It's bad enough that the bakers have to spend their days in such places; but then we've all become used to that and don't seem to mind it any longer, as if the baker was born for the cellar life. But not so the actor. For the first time in my life it suddenly occurred to me that the actors and actresses are not performing their antics of their own free will any more than I would be making waists just for the fun of it.

Here, again, I had to control myself and rush on with the sale—it was getting late. I had taken in a goodly sum of money, but wasn't satisfied with the day's work, so took a new supply and went up Broadway to meet the theater going crowds. I know better now. It only goes to show how little I still knew of life, especially in that part of the city. The vultures in human shape were out for prey and the streets in that neighborhood were no place for a woman. My first impulse was to turn back, but the money is needed so badly that I made up my mind to be deaf to all sorts of insinuations, and I stayed and heard words that I hope never again to hear in my life. I saw women ready to exchange their honor for a few cents or a meal. Venerable gentlemen, perhaps fathers of large families, paying the price. Young men escorting their ladies to theaters and at the same time flirting with the girls on the corner. But what of it, even if it did make my blood boil in me and my head ache as if it would split, us girls had sold thirty-five thousand papers and took in more than five thousand dollars?

Ray and I are sure to get three dollars apiece. That means five dollars for Mrs. Bloom's landlord and a whole dollar for bread. One can buy twenty five-cent loaves for that.

December 31

A human sandwich! Yes, that's precisely what I was today. I wonder why in heaven people look with such contempt at the unfortunates who have to make a living that way? To tell the truth, I really do not know why they are worse than the gay actress or the school teacher or anybody else who's trying to make a living by honest work.

After all, I don't know whether it is harder to put on two boards with large letters written upon them and thus parade the streets, or stand up on a brightly-lit stage and sing and dance while your heart is, perhaps, breaking from some secret sorrow.

I must say I've become a different being; I can't look upon things with the same eyes I used to. I don't seem to distinguish any longer what is respectable and what ain't. I don't see why the baker is worse than the doctor—both help prolong human life.

It seems to me that everybody ought to be willing to do what's right and that's just why I pinned on my chest and back those two large posters, picked up a bundle of Calls under my arm and promenaded up and down Twenty-third street for more than two hours. By doing this I've accomplished a double purpose—I've advertised the Sunday meeting and given the public to understand that us girls won't stop before anything if it is for the good of the cause.

And sure enough, whom should I come across but Mr. Hayman! "Mary, is it possible that you've come down so low?" exclaimed the gentleman, evidently pained at my appearance.

I just told him that the success of our fight is more important than any personal humiliation. Then added: "Think of it, Mr. Hayman, and when you get home put it in your pipe and smoke it."

They can stand on their head, but there ain't no use—they'll have to give in after all. "How vulgar," murmured a lady coming out from one of the stores. She was dressed to kill and under her arm she carried a little puppy.

It's strange how widely different our views are. She thought it vulgar to fight for a noble cause and I think it's more than vulgar, in fact, criminal, to pay thousands for little puppies, carry them about, fondle them and surround them with all sorts of comforts, while thousands of little children are dying for want of proper care.

I really felt sorry for that swell. From morning until night and from night until morning she doesn't think of a blessed thing but herself, until she's about sick and tired of her own person and for want of anything better turns to dogs.

A few minutes later a gentleman remarked that us girls are too anxious to gain notoriety. He wanted to assure me that the best woman is the one of whom neither good nor bad is ever heard outside of her own home.

I do wish the people would stop sending us to homes which we ain't got. What if we do make ourselves notorious? If we can't gain the people's attention any other way, then let it be through notoriety. There wasn't a person that passed me this morning but stopped long enough to read the poster and that's just what I wanted.

Met Jim near Fifth avenue. He came right over, greeted me in the most friendly way and walked alongside of me as if nothing was the matter, as if it was perfectly natural for me to do what I was doing. He seemed to approve of my rig. I must say, but the world does change!

The landlord kicked like a steer. He won't hear of being satisfied with five dollars; said that he don't buy houses for charity, but to get all the money he can out of them. I believe him. This cry for money is sickening. As if they're the happier for having lots of it? They wanted to know at the League if I was going out on picket duty tomorrow. Why, to be sure I am, and Jim's coming along with me.

January 1, 1910

I was so tired from the day's work that I didn't even know when the New Year was ushered in. And another thing, the people in our neighborhood do not celebrate. As Mrs. Bloom justly said this morning: "A new year means new sorrow. It seems to grow with time," and the poor woman shook her head mournfully. "There ain't a bit of coal in the house, mother," called to her Sammy at that moment. The kid was numb from cold and was anxious to start a fire. The unfortunate mother bit her lips hard so as not to burst out crying and left the house, making believe she didn't hear what the boy said.

The first time I witnessed such a scene I nearly went daffy. I couldn't understand why Mrs. Bloom ran out of the house. But now I'm getting used to it—it's almost an everyday affair, and I don't know as Mrs. Bloom can be blamed for running off—she can't simply listen to the children's pitiful wail.

I left the house without being able to heat up a bit of water and moisten my dried-up lips. I felt real wretched, but as I neared the Bijou I spied Jim in the distance. Something of the old thrill passed through me. It's the greatest joy in life to meet Jim nowadays—we have so much to say to each other. Jim spends his evenings reading and then tells me all about the things he finds in these numerous books and pamphlets he has been buying of late. At times he is puzzled about one thing or another and then I apply my knowledge from the book of life.

As we stood there talking Jim noticed that Fanny was surrounded by a couple of thugs, who were insulting the child in the most unspeakable terms. Without a thought of personal danger my brave boy knocked the two of them down. He was just furious at the police, who jabber so much about purifying the city.

"Mary," said he to me as I was dragging him away from further trouble, "this outrageous treatment of our women is an everlasting shame upon the heads of every citizen of this great city. In the South they put a noose about a man's neck for insulting a woman. Here we've grown so callous and cold-blooded that we take it as a joke."

While I pleaded with him to cool down I felt happy at the thought of the wonderful change in my own Jim.

Unable to remain near the Bijou that day, I took hold of

Jim's sleeve and gently led him away from mischief. Gradually his indignation calmed down a bit and he turned his attention on something I had told him about the scene at Mrs. Bloom's.

"Mary," said Jim, and he blushed like a girl, "why can't we eat our lunch with the Blooms? We can buy all the stuff on our way there." This was the first time since I left home that he was asking permission to visit my new abode. It ain't that I didn't want him to, but I felt a bit nervous. I was ashamed to take him through the filthy yard which leads to the house, then up the narrow, dilapidated stairway and into Mrs. Bloom's gloomy, half-dark kitchen, where in spite of the bitter cold the air is just stifling.

Jim must have guessed the cause of my embarrassment, for he said: "I think it will take some time before the best of you women will get rid of your false pride. Suppose you do live in a wretched place, what of it? Poverty may be a curse, but it's nothing to be ashamed of."

Who would have thought this of Jim? But then I may as well say, who would have thought this of me? Perhaps it's only natural that it should be so; it's only inevitable that the human mind should keep growing once it's brought into action.

Make believe the little Blooms weren't delighted with the feast we gave them.

"Mary, you've a fine steady," they said to me when Jim left the house this evening. I tell you what, it's simply amazing to hear those kids talk—they're just like little old men and women. Poor kids! I feel sorry for them. They will never know the meaning of childhood—they never had any; they are born old. Why should this world be made up of such contrasts, I wonder? Here's us American children who act like kids even when they grow up and there's them that worry and suffer from the very cradle. Jim's company made me happy for a while and I hope I'll get some good rest tonight.

January 2

I'm beginning to think that if us girls make up our minds to see a thing succeed we are bound to have it so. The Carnegie meeting was even greater than us girls expected it to be. But I must say we worked for it. I left the house this morning much earlier than usual in order to make the round of the different halls and impress upon the girls the necessity of making this affair a howling success.

In every meeting room I encountered almost one and the same picture—girls divided into small groups talking earnestly about their sad plight and the seeming hopelessness of settlement in the near future. I must say, though, that all were deeply interested in the subject. There were many who balked against the decision to hold out still longer, having done their duty for so many weeks, they were now getting tired and I don't know as any one could be very severe with them for feeling that way.

But those who had once felt the grip of a policeman's hand on their shoulder were among the staunchest advocates of staying out to the last. As I listened to their discussions I felt glad the police were so generous in their treatment of us girls—their action was the best eye-opener. A day in jail and a girl couldn't help but realize the injustice of it all.

I was all tired out by seven o'clock, but had no time to stop and think of it. There was still plenty of work ahead; we had to get the girls that were arrested upon the platform and there muster them out according to the degree of abuse they had suffered. It's easy to say—six hundred of us arrested girls, a bunch of innocent girls arrested and placed on trial during these long weeks of battle for the crime of refusing to work for starvation wages!

I think that this meeting was the best ever—by the expression of the audience it was clear that it was appalled by the sight of us grouped together on that brightly-lit stage and justly indignant at those who were responsible for our suffering. Why, even I myself felt it more when I saw it right before my eyes— rows upon rows of young girls with the brunt of imprisonment printed on their chest. It's terrible, this sudden confronting of facts. A body can't help shrinking from a society where such a thing is possible. I know I had to; I was fairly sick at the sight of all those silent witnesses and I can imagine the effect it had upon strangers who did not know before the extent of the persecution.

The room went round and round me. I feared that I may faint and disturb that immense crowd, but luckily for me and the meeting I caught Jim's eye. It was full of devotion and encouragement, and made me feel as if a waft of fresh air had suddenly poured upon me and strengthened me in body and mind.

I must say that fate, which had originally brought Jim and me together, must look on and be proud of the result—Jim is my mainstay nowadays. Having entered the path of truth through different channels we are constantly drawing nearer to each other. I now realize that life will be worth living when we finally join our hands and hearts in order to support one another in life's struggle.

The speeches! I don't see how anybody could listen to them and remain calm. It seems to me that all those present must have left the hall determined to see justice done to us sufferers. But as good as the speeches were, the climax was reached when that little Jew girl appeared on the stage. She looked so small and her voice sounded so childish that everybody gasped for breath—to think that she had been for a day in that wretched place called the workhouse! Poor kid! she tried hard to tell the audience why she was sent there, but succeeded in uttering a few words only and these so pathetic that even our own girls had to cry.

As the evening progressed I glanced occasionally at Jim and in the fullness of my heart I saw once more the dear, faultless, idolized man I had worshipped a while ago. The intervening few weeks had slipped from my memory. The unspoken tie which had bound us before, as if we were husband and wife already, was born anew. Unknown to myself I burst into passionate tears, but they were only tears of joy and hope for the future.

January 3

I think the backbone of the Bosses' Union is broken, though they wouldn't acknowledge it and keep up a brave front. The strike isn't as yet declared off and may not be for many days to come. But one by one their members come quietly to the union office, sign their agreements and take back their old workers.

God! what a satisfaction it is to see them do it. What a world of self-respect every new surrender gives us girls. This wholesale desperation gives the scab bosses the chill—they send their girls by the flock to the League to take out their union cards. Was there ever heard before a similar victory? And all because us girls kept pulling together and not on opposite sides, as most working people are wont to do. Just because we've made up our mind to stand and fall together.

I couldn't say that it was an easy thing, either. When I look at our girls or at the League women I only realize the terrific effort we've all made. As I come to think of my first entrance into this battle I can't help wondering at the amount of knowledge I've gained. I was but a silly girl rushing in for the thirst of fun in me, staying with them at the dictates of my heart and not my head, and finally reasoning it all out for myself.

I would just love to know if the people at large have at last learned the necessity of our organization, the impossibility of avoiding this strike. It ain't that I really care what they think, I should stick to the girls at any rate; but it's for the sake of those who are to follow us.

If I'd consult my personal interest I'd join hands with Jim at once, but not now, not while the girls are still fighting. Their pale, joyless faces would haunt me to my very grave. My suffering may make it easier for others to earn a living in the long run.

Mrs. Bloom told me of a neighbor who cut off her long hair and sold it for five dollars. Poor Mrs. Bloom! for the first time in her life she deplored the fact of being deprived of long tresses. Another woman had pulled off two gold crowns from her teeth and sold them for bread. It sounds more like a novel, but I'm sorry to say it ain't; it's as much of a fact as our general suffering.

Mr. Hayman met me again yesterday as I was going to Carnegie Hall and offered to take me as a sample maker on a fifteen dollar per week salary steady. I just told him that it ain't for myself that I'm fighting, but for Ray and Rose and Jenny. To think of it, fourteen-year-old Jenny has to work at flower-making for just twenty-five cents a day! And she doesn't make it all during the day, either—we help her at night.

It ain't no easy job, this flower-making ain't. The kid's fingers are all pricked and swollen, then the dye gets into them and they fester like anything. But even this ain't as bad as Minnie's work. She just recovered from her sickness and some one got tassels for her to make. Talk about a merciful world! where does the mercy come in I don't know. Here is her that can scarcely breathe as it is, blowing from morning until night, for this is the only way of parting the numerous threads of silk that go to make up a single tassel.

Minnie is eager to make some money; she knows what her illness meant to the family and wants to make some amends for it. And it ain't the money alone—the girl wants to run away from her thoughts or she'd land where Lilly did. She had to be put in a straitjacket—her mind had given way under the terrible strain. In ain't no surprise, either. What else can follow in the wake of abuse and starvation but suicide and insanity? To tell the truth, of the two I would prefer the first.

Well, well, quite a pleasant subject I have dwindled to. I didn't know it until I just glanced at the note book. People say all roads lead to Rome, and with us girls everything seems to center around struggle and suffering. Here we are, thousands of us, for many weeks past, from morning until night, thinking, talking and working for nothing but the strike. And yet, I'm never tired to keep it up. The strike to me is like a many colored rainbow, each color presenting a new food for study. All the suffering and ugliness I'm surrounded with have done me a great service.

January 4

Took a flying trip out of town and did it in a parlor car at that, but this ain't the best of it, either. I came back with a check for a thousand dollars made out to the treasurer of the union. This money came from hard-working men and women who spend many long hours in the sweating dens of our large cities. It was donated to us girls by the convention of the International Ladies' Garment Workers' Union.

As soon as our train left the city early this morning and sped out into the broad, open field I felt a heavy cloud lifted off my shoulders. It was real good to see the blue sky and white, snow-covered fields and mountains. I thought of our girls and wished I could take them all along with me and give them a chance to breathe freely for once in their life. How many of them are pining away in the close, stifling air of our big city, where the buildings are growing ever taller, the number of people larger and the ways of earning a living harder.

I felt like a forlorn sheep at first. I must have acted queer, for I noticed a grin on almost every face that was turned toward me. It made me real mad—it's all good and well for them that's got nothing else to do to know all the traveling etiquettes, but how in the world is one of us to know all these things—the hard work is enough to crush everything out of one's head.

To avoid their persistent glances I rose and wanted to enter the ladies' dressing room, but landed in the porters' quarters instead. It gives me a chill even now when I think of the half a dozen dark grinning faces. In anger I rushed back to my seat and buried my head in the window. I just longed for Jim and his good counsel.

Suddenly my ear was attracted by the conversation of two men, evidently salesmen. One claimed that the judges were treating us girls too mildly. What made him furious was the fact that the darned foreigners had not a bit of consideration for an American soul whose expenses run as high as eight dollars per day, cigars alone amounting to one fifty.

This conversation was something new again—no wonder us girls have to work for so little when the go-betweens spend that much. What must the boss himself be spending?

The delegation at the convention did not tend to raise my spirits, except for their good will and the money they voted to give us. But, honestly, I felt guilty to take it away from them— they looked, at least most of them, as if they never get a full meal.

I had to make my appeal for sympathy on behalf of those whose misery I have been a partner to, but even as I spoke I watched their stooped shoulders, their thwarted growth; they looked the typical overworked beings they are described to be.

For whom and for what do they waste their lives away? Their families don't get much out of their work, they themselves get still less; then where does it all go, this work of theirs? I—I don't know, but these thoughts drive me nigh crazy at times. These people are all self-supporting, honest and good to their kind—why should they be deprived of leading a decent life?

It was almost two o'clock when I got out of the convention. In a hurry to catch my train I rushed into the nearest lunch-room to get a bite, for I felt faint. It was an immense place where the sales and office girls take their lunch. It's amazing how quickly they do it. I wondered that they don't burn their insides with the boiling coffee, for they get through with the entire performance in less than five minutes with the waiting upon themselves and all. Of course, they don't eat anything to speak of—how can they? A girl can hardly spend more than fifteen cents for lunch, while some of them can't spend even that much, and what does a body get now for that money? The pity of it is that those hundreds of girls I watched there at that lunch counter were perfectly ignorant of their own condition, just as I was two months ago. I'm sure they would have had a good laugh at my expense had I tried to explain things to them.

It gave me the chills to listen to their talk—their whole existence is bent on imitating the rich. The train is nearing town; I will have to stop.

January 5

I was glad to get back. After all, there ain't no place like little old New York. And, to tell the truth, I think it's all Jim's fault. Dear old boy! He was waiting impatiently for me at the station. I knew he hated to see me go, but he wouldn't stand between me and the welfare of the strike for anything in the world.

And everybody takes him at his right worth. Mrs. Bloom said to me the other morning: "Mary, you're the hardest person I've come across. What ails you, girlie? The girls trust you with their affairs; you're loved by the kindest man livin' and needn't go hungry if you don't want to. Then why go around as if the world's sorrows rest upon your shoulders?"

It may be true enough, but how can a body be happy amidst all this misery; one insignificant little tree in this great forest of suffering people? To tell the truth, I don't think there's such a thing as a perfectly happy person nowadays; it seems that every one of us has some skeleton hid away deep in his heart.

When I got to the League Mary asked me to attend a conference. I was sure that we were going to get some money out of it and went. But it proved to be one of those fake affairs held by our supposed-to-be friends for the purpose of forming a new organization that would make it its business to drive the Socialists out of the union movement. If I hadn't felt so sad in general there was an opportunity for some good fun. It was to laugh the way those swell ladies were worrying about the welfare of us working girls.

"Why, they've been completely neglected by us," pleaded Eve, the temptress. "And the horrid Socialists lost no opportunity to enlighten them about the principles of Socialism. What will become of us if this is permitted to go on? We must at once start some systematic work in order to educate the girls out of Socialism." I guess she'll have a hard job.

Big strong Ann, who's got more money than she can count, sat there and continually nodded her head in approval of what Eve had to say. I would just love to make her roll up her sleeves and do an honest day's work, like us girls have to do all the time. I'll bet you ten to one that our union wouldn't seem too radical to her then.

"Labor conditions are too serious a matter," said one of the painted ladies. "Especially now," she added. "When living costs so much the Socialists are liable to light a terrible fire of revolt." I honestly wish they would.

"Those Socialists are dangerous," chimed in another, who has been changing her charitable occupations and husbands more frequently than some people do their clothes, and was therefore considered an authority on both subjects. "Their principles go to bring about the disruption of the home," continued the worthy matron.

I felt just like telling them that our homes can no longer be disrupted, for the most of us working people have no homes, but my opinion wasn't asked and I kept mum. I've gone through too much to care for their jabbering; it's only that they're trying their best to make trouble. I wouldn't be at all surprised if they'd be glad to see the League go to the dogs, but not on your life—we've too many good fighters in there.

As Pauline said to me: "It's just because I have that bigger ideal in view that I can work with such a devotion. If I didn't believe that this struggle is only the first step on the road to freedom I don't know as I could keep it up in spite of all the obstacles in my way."

I shouldn't wonder but that some day Jim and I will land in the same boat with Pauline and the rest of them who see greater hope for us working people than the mere winning of this strike, which may after all be lost again, even before we've time to say Jack Robinson.

One could hardly believe it, but Jim's getting stronger on that point than I am. "See here," he said to me when we left Carnegie Hall, "I think us working people are the stupidest ever; what's the use of making so much fuss against these judges now when it's too late; why in the world can't we stop sending them where they do not belong?"

January 6

I wonder why they've brought us down to the Tombs, unless they've come to look upon us girls as upon terrible criminals? It gives me the shivers to hear the grating of the iron doors. I feel as though the thick gray walls are drawing much closer and closer upon me. Their grayness is entering my very bones. They seem so old as if they were here from the beginning of the world. And the terrible, mysterious halls which lead one into a dark unknown distance, perhaps hell itself, where the shadows of all those that were here before us are still roaming about.

Lord! when we left the street the day was bright and sunny, but in this miserable place it feels as if the sun never shines. And I must say it's precious little that a body can feel within these high stone fences. One can hardly believe that there is such a thing as life, joy and happiness.

I'm that scared that I could yell at the top of my voice, if it would only break this horrible silence. And yet, strange as it may seem, I ain't a bit surprised at being here. I took it for granted when I was being dragged into a patrol wagon once more, for I knew all along that it was coming. This time the police had a fine crop—fifteen of us girls at one grab. But, to tell the truth, I'm more mad at that fluffy thing who was the cause of our arrest than I am at the cops.

As if we ain't got enough trouble; no, she need come down to show off before her fellow how brave she can be—anything to pass the time away. And why not? She didn't lose anything by it—had all the excitement she was looking for, posed as a martyr, had a dozen or more pictures taken free of charge and was then taken home by her rich pa. I'm sure she's now sittin' in one of them swell hotels eating a good supper and talking of the great deed—great, to be sure—to leave us in a lurch. It's on account of her that we'll have to stay here over night, for she had the trial postponed until tomorrow. I think it's a shame; it was she that started it all. I'm pretty sure none of the Jew girls would be that mean. And when I come to think of it, what did she do for us girls all these weeks, and yet the papers were full of her. They say she's goin' to be a lawyer; well I'm sure that this free advertising will pay her, for it will mean business in the end. Talk about the Jews being shrewd in the business line—I think our Americans can beat them all hollow.

My hand is numb from cold; I can hardly see how to scribble these lines, but then, anything not to remain still. Poor Jim! I'm sure he'll feel even worse than I do, but it'll do him good in the long run. It will strengthen his spirit of rebellion, for we really can't feel a thing until it comes right near home. I'm sure Jim's sorry for all the girls and would do anything in his power to put a stop to these outrages, and yet it would be so different when he knows that I'm the one who is made to suffer.

This is perhaps one of the reasons why I'm so mad at that fluffy thing. If her sympathy for us hadn't been skin deep, if she had really cared for us girls the way we do for each other she would have remained with us. This more than anything else would have made her kind realize the horrors we girls are subject to. And I'm certain something would have been done.

But I really don't know as I ought to excite myself over it. I guess it's just because I'm hungry and Ray's sittin' in the corner crying to break her heart, and the other girls can't be much better off than we are. The most of them, like myself, are under arrest for the third time and are sure to be sent to the workhouse. And it ain't that I'm such a coward, but it means additional worry for the union; it stops them from attending to the strike proper, and that's just what our bosses want.

I wish they'd let us lie down at least. I feel as though some one has given me a good clubbing—well, the cops weren't a bit gentle in handling us girls. This time they've treated us like equals with the men criminals. It's funny, when we do something wrong or are blamed for doing something we didn't do we are punished like men, but when we want to have our say we ain't as good as they are.

January 7

And so this is the second day of my prison life; it seems almost a century since that woman first came in to fix us for the night. "Get out of my way," she growled, when Ray and I attempted to ask her a question. She was one of the trusted prisoners and looked upon us new ones with a feeling of superiority.

She unstrapped the board that had been fastened to the wall, pulled out from behind it a couple of dirty blankets, then climbed upon it, did the same to the upper board and ordered us to bed. I was mighty glad; I didn't know what was awaiting me after I'd get there. It's a good thing Ray was afraid to sleep alone and nestled close by me—it helped a bit. I ain't a nervous lady, but I think the strongest man must needs get the shivers at the sight of all them rats—they crawled around the cot, scratched upon the walls and squealed loud enough to bring the evil one out of his hiding place.

I left off writing this morning in order to eat my breakfast, but before I took a couple of mouthfuls I was called into the prison office. God! I thought that the rats and vermin were bad enough, but the questions they asked me down there beat it all.

I suppose that's what people call the sweatin' box—well, I didn't sweat; I turned as cold as a piece of ice—who were they to ask of my heart's secrets, to suggest things that were enough to bring blushes and tears to the most depraved being? It was just maddening to think that I was completely in their power. I felt as though the room was reeling before me, my brain refused to work and I answered their questions like one in a dream.

Luckily for me it was getting high time to go to court, and a guard took me across the Bridge of Sighs. The Bridge of Sighs—I've often read about it, but that isn't to be on it, to see the thousands of people rushing past, each stopping long enough to cast a pitiful, sneering or defying gaze in the direction of those who have sinned in the eyes of the law. I felt sick at heart; it pained me to see the look of despair in the eyes of the prisoners who were being led across like myself. I couldn't help feeling with them and against all those curious ones who come to enjoy our misery. But, suddenly, amidst the sea of faces I spied a pair of clear bright eyes—they carried a message of love for me. I had barely time to intercept it when I was taken into the prisoners' pen. I guess this is about all I'll see of Jim today.

Us girls spent two hours in that close, stuffy room and were again taken across the bridge—fluffy's lawyer has postponed the trial for another day. I'm really surprised that nobody tries to bail us out, but I don't know as they, down at the union, can be blamed so much; they surely have their hands full. It's heartbreaking to see what this one day did to the girls. They look as if they'd been for weeks on a sickbed. And now that Ray is taken away from me I feel like a stray duckling. The other prisoners look sneeringly at my writing and I guess I'd better stop.

January 8

A nother wretched night, in fact, by far worse than the first—the woman above me would not stand for my tossing about, she had it in for me since the afternoon, and now thumped and growled like a mad cat. "Think of that swellness—this place ain't good enough for her. And suppose it ain't, your poor, dear darlin', there are others here, perhaps, as good as yourself."

I said nothing to her—what was the use—she was one of those creatures who are lost to all sense of reason; her yellow, shriveled-up face, her trembling hands and dull brazen eyes made me shrink from her in horror. She must have felt it at once and swore and cursed in the most unspeakable language. She had it in for everybody, her dead parents, her lost lover and still-born child, she hated them all and me with them.

It was terrible, terrible to see a young woman so deep down in the mud. I thought she'd drive me mad; I clutched at the boards of my bed to steady myself. "I ain't good enough for you," shouted my neighbor. "Wait until I get a chance at your hair—you'll see the stars flyin' in all directions." Here, luckily for me the guard entered and seeing her in convulsions dragged her out of the cell.

Her cursing helped me to forget the rats for awhile; it was now getting light and I knew they'd run back in the holes. I longed for some rest and peace, but this is not a thing prescribed for prisoners. Before I had a chance to turn around and doze off I was told it was time to rise. I'm tired, sleepy and miserable, but it's soon time to go to court. I do hope I'll know my fate today. I've come to think that the worst part in a prisoner's life is the suspense before the trial. It's wonderful what an expert I'm becoming of late. I truly think that I've been living at the rate of a year an hour, for I feel as though I'm a thousand years old.

"Young woman," said the judge to me sternly when I was at last brought before him this morning, "you are under arrest for the third time—remember that you were last released upon the promise to keep within the letter of the law."

"But I did, your honor," I replied in a firm manner. He didn't like my answer and warned me angrily: "Mind you, woman, you are committing perjury; you are on your oath. The officer here says you've disturbed the peace."

I was about to say something to him about those officers when I caught sight of fluffy, togged out in her best finery, two men at her side and a half dozen reporters back of her. I just hated them all that minute. What was the use of talking; no matter what I'd say won't do me any good. Talk about the law being equal for all, rich and poor alike. No fear of her goin' to the workhouse. It's us poor devils that'll have to pay the fiddler for all the fun she got out of us. I'm sure everybody in that courtroom knew I was innocent and yet, after a momentary silence, the judge said to me calmly: "Five days in the workhouse."

Poor Jim! I saw him all the while standing in a corner, his head bowed low, as if he dared not catch my eye. But when the judge pronounced sentence he looked up and almost reeled off his feet. I believe the boy is completely stunned by the turn of affairs.

The full meaning of the verdict didn't dawn upon him until he met me at the door when I was being led back to prison. There was such a pitiful look of anxiety in his eyes as he pressed my hand that I couldn't help throwing my hands around his neck and embracing him right there in front of everybody.

"How can they be so cruel to you, Mary?" he muttered in a choked voice, the tears trickling down his pale cheeks. "Mary," he continued, "you are doing your duty an' I shall do mine; while you're away I will do the picketing for you."

And now I'm back again for another night with the rats. To-morrow we'll be sent to the island. Meanwhile I haven't eaten for two days. It makes me sick to look at the so-called soup which they give us prisoners for dinner. I wouldn't give it to my pet dog, if I had any. I wonder if the time will ever come when prisons will be torn down, when all this greed, which is the cause of most of the crimes, will disappear altogether?

January 9

O h, it's terrible, terrible to look upon all these women in their striped dresses and heavy shoes. The word convict seems to be imprinted on their very forehead. Perhaps it's only my imagination. I wonder what I look like. I'd just love to get hold of a bit of mirror. I must be even worse than the rest, for my garb is twice as big as myself. The matron had to pin it up all around with pins or I couldn't make a step in it.

I must say that this is better after all than the miserable prison down on Center street. Here a body has at least space to breathe. Of course, the work is hard enough to kill a horse, the companions of the toughest kind, the matron far from being gentle, the rooms gray, gloomy and bare of furniture except a number of wooden benches and the work-tables. But when I think of the terrible filth I've left behind me I'm almost thankful for being here. And people say that we Americans have model prisons. I guess it's because they've never been serving time within them.

We got here shortly before noon and by the time my history was taken down and my clothes changed for the ones I'm wearing it was time to go for dinner. I wish we hadn't gone—I'm still sick to my stomach. I must say that hard as the work may be, the food is the worst part of the workhouse program. The tin dishes and spoons look as if they had been used by many, many miserable beings before us. The bread was made of nothing but bran and corn; the soup was even worse than the one at the Tombs, and I honestly believe that I'd rather starve to death than take another mouthful while I'm here. The potatoes were stale and sour, the gruel raw and all we tasted of beef was a horribly sickening smell.

The girls marched in the so-called dining-room in line like school children under the severe supervision of the matron. And this is the only time when they're supposed to be given some freedom, when they're allowed to exchange a word or two with each other. But at every attempt to make a jest, which I must say was not of the Sunday school order, she threatened and upbraided them. It really made me smile when we were ordered to say grace. What a clear, open lie. Whom do they want to blind by it? I'm sure not the girls, for they know better; they realize that it's precious little that they have to be thankful for. And the matron had the hardest time in getting one of the girls to say it aloud for the rest. Each one tried in turn to shove it off on the other until it fell to the lot of Dutch Annie—a child of scarcely more than sixteen. She lowered her long lashes and with her still pretty mouth commenced to chant the few well-known words. With bowed heads the diners giggled, nevertheless, at the earnest way in which Annie performed her task and were, of course, upbraided by the matron.

"I'd be blessed if I eat this stuff," said my neighbor, pushing aside her plate of soup. "I guess some one must be getting rich on us," she continued in a loud enough voice for the entire assembly to hear her.

"Hold your mouth," shouted our overseer, "or you'll have another dose of the darkroom." The girl turned pale and bent her head low over the table. I wonder what chamber of horrors that may be?

Within half an hour the girls were back at work and I was set to scrubbing. I'm surprised that the boards on the floors do not wear out from all the scrubbing they're getting. I think it's the worst punishment anybody could have invented. To go on day after day scrubbing floors without any purpose or reason for doing it. I ain't no educator nor reformer, but, somehow, I fail to see how in the world they expect us girls to turn a new leaf, to become better through the performance of this stupid job. What enlightenment is there in lying down on the floor, brush with rag in hand, and moving on one's knees to cover many feet of flooring, scrubbing, washing and drying, until every bone in the body aches?

I'm surprised at myself that I've still enough energy left to put down my thoughts on paper. But people often say that by long practice a habit becomes one's second nature, and I've come to think that this is perfectly true about my scribblin'. I've simply got to do it. I see the girls are rushing indoors and must stop. This was a bit of respite we get after supper—horrid black coffee without sugar and some more of the same bread.

January 10

Thank the Lord! Almost two of my five days in the workhouse gone. And mighty hard days at that. It was only half past seven when we were ordered to bed last night—that's the rule. No lights or talking after that. But picture a room full of women who have been kept silent the whole day long and are not permitted to say a word to one another after the daily labor is done. Of course they talk, even if they have to pay heavily for it.

I was glad to get to bed, hard as it was, but I couldn't fall asleep to save my life. "Why are you here?" I asked of the girl on a cot next to mine.

"I suppose for the very same reason that you are here," replied my neighbor.

The tone of her voice told the tale of her guilt. My face turned crimson and I shrank from the thought that every other woman in the room was here for the very same reason. I didn't want them to think that I, too, was one of them and snapped at her proudly; "I didn't want to work for starvation wages and struck; that's the crime I've committed."

"An' I couldn't go on livin' on starvation wages any longer and had to sell my body instead of my hands," said the girl calmly.

My first impulse was to turn away from the sinner. But who should be the judge of our conscience? Who has a right to blame the girl for what she turned out to be? It's hard to tell what the best of us would do when pressed real hard.

The poor devil was caught in the act of replying to me and was taken out of the room—I didn't see her since and feel a bit uneasy—it was my fault after all. I'd rather they had punished me in her stead—I've only three more days of it, while she has many months. I scarcely slept for the rest of that night. And with the first rays of sunshine we were made to rise, wash, clean up the beds and go down to breakfast—black coffee and bread.

After that came the scrubbing business once more. God! I'm so sore that I can hardly move about.

I thought that twelve o'clock would never come, but it did and with it the horrid, nasty leavings of yesterday's soup. Dutch Annie put me wise to it: "If you don't fill your bowl with bread crumbs and make a mush out of that stuff, we're sure to get it again tomorrow," she warned me.

Poor kid! I'm really sorry for her. She got a talkin' to while we were out in the yard and I think her mother is more to blame for what she is than the girl herself. Annie eloped with a man twice her age. The rascal left her soon after and when the girl conquered her shame and returned home, to tell it in her own words: "Ma, she lifted the broomstick at me and shouted that I must never again darken her door. An' I didn't. But you see," she added blushingly, "I was still green in the business and landed here instead of having a good time. But I'll be more careful when I come out of here."

"You don't mean to say that you'll return to the same life?" I said with a shudder.

"An' what else am I to do?" asked me the girl point blank. I had no advice or suggestion to give her. In fact I've come to think that sending a young sinner to the workhouse is the surest means of perpetuating her in her trade. Here she meets many women more experienced than herself, women who have tasted all the bitter sweetness of a fast life, and, encouraged by their stories and triumphs, she comes out of this miserable place anxious to get another taste of gay life, from which she was prevented while at the workhouse. Who can blame her for wanting to fill her stomach with some of the good things? Not one who knows what it is to live on prison food. Lord! my own insides are so shrunk together that I don't believe I'll ever again be able to eat a full meal. I don't really know how they can go on that way for months, unless one gets used to it, like every other suffering. I suppose some of them have long since lost the taste and it don't matter what they get so long as they stuff themselves full. The worst part for them is the drink they miss so much. It is almost pitiful to see the expression of despair on their distorted faces. Well, it's bedtime again.

January 11

Now I know where my neighbor had disappeared to the other night. I've been there since myself. When I went to bed last night I was startled by terrible, heartrending moans. The woman alongside of me was in agony. A part of her face was all eaten up by some terrible disease and the creature could find no relief from pain except in drugging herself, but this was denied to her here.

I couldn't bear to hear her suffer so, so I forgot all the strict orders and got down on my knees close to her trying to find out if there was anything I could do for her. A minute later a pair of strong hands were dragging me swiftly into the dimly lit hall, and from there down, down a narrow stairway. It seemed to have lasted a long, long while; my shoulders ached, my head felt dizzy, but finally I found myself in the darkroom. The so-much-dreaded darkroom where a body remains strapped down to a pole in a pitch-dark corner and must keep moving the feet all the while to frighten the many rats away.

I think I was more dead than alive when they took me out of there this noontime. Even our big, fat watchdog got scared at my looks and sent me up to the sewing room for the rest of the afternoon. This ain't much worse than our city workrooms, except that a body dare not murmur a word, if one don't care to spend a day in the darkroom. But as old Martha says: "If you are here long enough you get used even to that." Poor, old, disheveled Martha! She says she has lived sixty-eight years, sixty of which she has spent between the street and the workhouse. It's for different things, too, that she's been coming there all this while. This last time it is for nothing else but too much rum. But who are we to judge her for taking it? As she rightly says, she'd been dead long ago if not for the warm stuff. It's really the only consolation she's got in this wide world. The wretched soul cried bitterly as she told me her tale of woe. At the age of eight her mother died from consumption and her father took to drink. She was beaten, neglected and starved until she fell in with a woman of the streets and then, oh, so many things happened. I wonder when I'll have my fill at the tree of knowledge! Where were our good people and the law when Martha was left alone in the world?

And what is still worse—her tale is the tale of many inmates here. Depraved as they may seem to us, they still shed many unregarded tears. If the people were only to hear of their untold tales they would surely want to turn a new leaf in the book of laws and map out a different path for all these poor, helpless beings.

They are neglected, suffer, sin, and are punished according to our laws. But when their term is up the doors close upon them, leaving them once more without shelter and food. They stop for a brief moment and then fall again a prey to vice and sin.

It may seem strange, but I've thought very little of the strike and our girls for the last three days. I have an idea that for the present my little mite is needed right here. The very air seems to be saturated with past, present and future suffering. It seems to me that I can be of some use to these shrinking, shivering, hopeless beings. Perhaps my word of human sympathy will help them to bear the harsh, upbraiding speeches of the matron, the darkroom and the miserable food.

Ray got one of her bronchial spells and they took her over to the so-called hospital. I wish I could find out how she's getting along. I think it was a crime to send her here to perform such hard labor. Why in the world don't they have some medical examination? I guess it's because they don't care what happens to the people sent here.

Two more days after this, but, silly as it may seem, I wish I could stay a while longer with them. As a part of the big forest of people I consider myself in a way responsible for their misery and degradation. It's us that live in sheltered homes that can still do something to put a stop to this terrible plague— they who are afflicted with it are too ill to attend to themselves. I'm mighty glad that I've the perseverance to jot down my thoughts. I shall try to make use of them some day.

January 12

This morning I went up to the sewing room to finish my yesterday's job. I was still tired from the experience in the darkroom and scarcely slept last night—I couldn't help thinking of Ray. She's got heart disease for one thing, and then this bronchial trouble.

"How's Ray?" I inquired of the matron when she came over to examine my work. I knew that questions weren't allowed, but I could no longer restrain myself. The matron gave me a stern look and turned to the next girl, but a moment later she came back and said: "She ain't a bit strong, but then she'll be out in another day."

"This may be too long a time," was my reply and I pleaded with our overseer to please let me see Ray for a brief moment. I was encouraged by the former's evident note of sympathy and hoped to obtain some relief for my suffering friend.

I know better now. "See here, young woman," the matron exclaimed, "no one is allowed to speak at work and I don't see any occasion for your doing so. If you keep up this chatter you'll go back to scrubbing."

"Oh, the poor creature must feel so lonely," I sobbed in frenzy.

"Pshaw!" sneered the matron. "We don't propose to stand for any scenes in this place," and with these words she raised me bodily from the bench and out into the hall I went. A few minutes later I was once more on my knees scrubbin', scrubbin', and mingling the soap water with my blood tears.

I was crying and thinking, thinking more than I ever did before in my life. How long were we going to suffer in this manner? Here was poor, unfortunate Ray living in a Christian land and yet slowly sacrificed on the altar of greed. And Dutch Annie and miserable old Martha and the thousands upon thousands of others, whose cry of despair had reached my ears at that moment. And as these unbearable thoughts crossed my brain I sobbed aloud. A hard punch between my ribs cut the thread of my thought and killed every vestige of hope which I still cherished about my seeing Ray before we are released.

I have my doubts if she will ever leave this place alive. God!

Just to think of Mrs. Bloom if this should happen. What in the world will she do? How will she be able to bear it all? I know how she suffered before this. As I've lived with her day by day I marveled at her wonderful patience with which she bore the heavy burdens; she ain't the kind that bends, but this is sure to break her.

I really don't know how I have lived through this long morning, but then, I had my revenge during the noon hour. Big strong Lina broke loose and didn't she lay it into that watchdog of ours. It all started at the dinner table when Lina found a piece of bread floating around in her soup.

"I ain't no dog to eat other people's leavings," she shouted at the top of her voice.

"Hold your mouth shut," warned her the matron.

As if by magic the girls all dropped their spoons and centered their eyes on the distinguished pair, who resembled two angry roosters. The matron thought to frighten Lina with her bossy eye, but the other wasn't of the timid kind either.

"Are you deaf?" shouted the matron, coming close to her. But Lina must have been waiting for her to do so. In an instant, before the other dogs had time to get near them, she threw her opponent down on the floor and gave her a few digs with the feet.

I could have laughed and cried at the sight. Lina settled some of our accounts, but we all knew what it meant for her. Nobody touched a morsel of food after the rebel was dragged out of the room. Rough, callous and degraded as these women are, they still have a human heart hidden under the unpleasant surface; they all felt with and for their kind, or as some of the Socialist speakers had told us, they, these wretched beings, were class conscious.

We worked on for the rest of the afternoon as if there was a corpse in our midst. I didn't hear anything about Ray. Perhaps she is—I won't, I won't say the word, but will tomorrow ever come?

January 13

Here I am back again at Mrs. Bloom's and Ray home with me. I don't really know why, but it seems like a dream, my arrest, the Tombs and the workhouse. Somehow I can't think of anything just now but Jim's words of love. Lord! but that man does love me. I'm almost afraid to think of all the happiness in store for me; I don't think it's right. And yet his passionate greeting made life worth living once more; it drove away the gloom cast upon me by the experience and association of the last few days.

"Jim, I'm hungry," were the first words I said to him. I knew it was stupid of me, but I hadn't anything decent to eat for almost a week. Jim didn't mind it a bit; he took me and Ray down to one of them big restaurants and ordered everything they had on hand. It must have broke him, for he ain't no millionaire by any means. Still, I didn't care. We ate and ate and ate, until we almost burst.

I hear Ray's coughing again. I wonder if it's from the food. I know her eyes were bigger than her stomach; she took more than it was good for her. And now she's in for the rest of the night. God! That dry, hollow cough sends a chill through my body. It sounds terrible in this death-like stillness. But my feeling ain't nothing as compared with the suffering it causes her mother. Poor woman! When they're all asleep she hides herself in a corner of the kitchen and weeps her aching heart away.

I asked Jim to pay my rent for me today, and don't know as I ought to be ashamed for doing it. I couldn't very well remain here without paying, not that she would object, but because I have a conscience and I ain't ready to go yet. Am determined to stick it out until Hayman settles. Why, it would be a terrible sin to leave Mrs. Bloom and Ray and the other girls just now, when they're worse off than ever. But I don't know any more when this strike will end—it seems to be everlasting—bosses keep settling every day in the week and yet I was told at the league this afternoon that there are four thousand still out.

The league women are just crazy for Jim, and no wonder; he was of more help to them this week than I would have been. Took off a week from his job and worked for us girls. It's really marvelous when I come to think of the turn affairs took in my life.

Jim said father was ripping mad when he heard of my plight. Said that I had disgraced him forever, but Jim didn't mince words with him—just told him what he thought of the entire treatment of me and promised to change my name as soon as I would be willing to do so. The minute Jim spoke these words the truth of what he wanted to say flashed upon my mind. "Jim, dear," said I quietly, "won't you marry me when Mr. Hayman settles with us girls?"

I wonder what my former friends would think of me if they'd hear that I proposed to Jim. But where's the wrong in it? Jim asked me to be his wife and I refused. Then why not be honest and tell him that I've changed my mind?

But Jim didn't think it out of the way one bit. "Yes," he said quickly, before I even had a chance to finish. "I'll marry you on the day your girls go back to work." Here he made me promise to go with him and take out a license, just to have it handy in case of necessity.

We talked and talked; there seemed to be no end of things to talk about. Jim, too, had occasion to become better acquainted with our girls and he praised them quite a little. Everybody knows him as Mary's Jim. And he says he ain't a bit ashamed of it.

"Mary," said Jim to me after we had talked a while about our future life, "I don't know as I could be called a woman's rights man, but it seems to me that these women ought to try and wake up us men as well. I know this little woman," pointing at me, "did wake me up. I've come to believe that us men do not understand the make-up of you girls. For we would know better if we did. It's silly talk; we can't live without one another; there can't be no man's nor woman's world, Mary, there must be a human world."

I just wonder what pa would say if he heard Jim talk. Lord! I'm so tired that the pen almost falls out of my hands.

January 14

Jim came bright and early this morning; said he was afraid he'd miss me. I knew by his looks that he hadn't slept a wink this night. He later told me that he couldn't get over the luck that had fallen to his share. I remember I heard some one say, "He loves best who prays best," but I'd say he loves best who thinks most. Jim could have never known such a love in his former state of mind. And that's just what he, himself, admitted to me today. "Mary," says he, "I couldn't commence to tell you how different my feeling for you is today from what it was two months ago. I then thought that I was a mighty oak and you the clinging ivy that would wind around me. Today, Mary, I know better—I understand that the soft clinging ivy is at times apt to suffocate the strong giant, while another oak of equal power standing side by side with me can only bring additional shelter and shade for my future prosperity."

I honestly believe that I must hurry and catch up with Jim or I'll be left behind before I know it. He seems to be learning things by leaps and bounds. But the beauty of it is that he don't keep anything to himself; he always tries to share his knowledge with me.

Promised to go up and visit the musicians' union this morning and took Jim as the other partner; we might as well begin our partnership at once. I knew he was anxious to go down to the City Hall and it may have been cruel of me to keep him back, but then duty comes before pleasure, at least to the soldiers in the ranks. And to tell the truth, I don't ever want to be a captain; somehow or other, willingly or not, a body is apt to get spoiled.

Coming back to the musicians' union. If I had my choice I'd rather call them a corporation than a union—at any rate they act that way. I got sick of the string of red tape they gave me. Just told them right out: "If you are too stingy to help us girls, why don't you say so?" The idea of their putting me off for two weeks. And what are we to do until then? I do hope the strike will be over by that time. I, at least, have no appetite to meet them once more.

I felt rather queer when we got to the City Hall around 1 o'clock. Marriage is rather a complicated affair and though I wasn't married to Jim as yet, this public announcement meant just as much to me as the latter ceremony will.

Jim and I do know each other and seem to understand each other's nature, and yet there seems to be such a world of difference between the life of a man and that of a woman that it's always a question how it will turn out in the end—this merging of two beings into one common life.

I looked rather shabbily dressed for a bride, but then most of my clothes is gone and what was the use of dressing up—had to go picketing in the afternoon?

I think it's a silly performance, this taking out of a permit to get married. Whom does it concern but the parties that are directly involved. I'd much rather have given the dollar to the union than to the clerk at the desk, and many more were the dollars they took in on that day. I was surprised to see that so many people want to get married on one and the same day.

Perhaps it's the best that they do—a few less girls suffering in loneliness. It ain't no easy thing to be a lady boarder in a room as small as a cage and as cold as an icebox. The man goes out, meets friends, takes in a show or two; but a girl, if she ain't of the gay kind, wastes her years away between the shop and the hall bedroom.

I got a-talking to one of the girls down there while we were waiting. The poor kid didn't look more than sixteen, though she said she was eighteen. She had left her mother and father on the other side and came over here alone. It wasn't long before she met this fellow. He ain't very old, either, but somehow I didn't like his looks. I sort of fear that he ain't marrying her for good. I couldn't help pitying the girl—here she's getting ready to become a wife and mother without the least thought about the grave duties she was about to accept. She kept fiddling with her wedding ring, which was hanging on a ribbon around her neck, and saying that she was so happy. I doubt if she knew what the word meant.

January 15

It seems that excitements will never cease with us—a new wrinkle today, an injunction. Well, well! who ever heard the like of it? I know I didn't. Was trying hard to find out the meaning of the word, but it seems to have as many different definitions as there are people in this wide world.

One says it's to assure order, the other to prevent it. One claims it's for the benefit of the working people so as to keep them within respectable bounds; others say it's to gag the working people.

I, for one, don't see where its usefulness or justice comes in. Taking, for instance, the one we were served with—it's nothing but a mean trick to keep us from walking on the sidewalks and talking to anybody we wish to. If this ain't gag law I don't know what is. To tell the truth, I think that them judges and their henchmen (the shyster lawyers) have gone a bit too far. The strings are liable to break and then—the Lord save them from the women!

We didn't worry very much. What is an injunction after all? A piece of paper. We crushed it into our pockets and went on to picket as usual. Them judges don't know what sort of people they're dealing with, when they make an attempt to shut up the League women. They can't understand what it means to devote one's life to an ideal. I'm almost inclined to believe that our women wouldn't fear death itself, not to speak of a police court sentence.

We had lots of fun down there on Walker street this morning. Here we were, every one of us that was served with an injunction to keep away from that neighborhood and there stood a pack of common dogs, placed there for the purpose of disturbing the peace. But instead of our being afraid of them, they seemed to be stupefied at our daring. It's because they're the sort of animals that bark as long as you don't show them a stick and give them to understand that you can fight back. But once they see that you're ready to defy them they commence to crawl. God! if only our workingmen were as brave as the women—the tables would surely be turned.

I'm sorry I couldn't see all the fun; had to rush off; was booked to speak before a lot of college girls. And thus it happened that for the first and, perhaps, for the last time in my life I went to college. But I wouldn't hear of going again. I had an idea that there ain't no worse snob than the young college snob and didn't think my words would have much weight with the girls, so Elsie went along with me.

But the world does change, I must say. Who would have thought of it only one short year ago. Here was I a plain, ordinary shop girl, with scarcely any education at all, sitting there on that high platform among many wise professors and looking down upon hundreds of well-to-do college girls who have spent their lifetime on books and study. And all because we woke up and fought for our rights. Respect yourself, and others are sure to follow suit. I do think that the working people as a whole would be better off if they had some self respect.

I was mighty glad to hear that old professor give the girls a piece of his mind. He just came right out with the goods—told them that they needn't think themselves better, nobler and brighter than us working girls. That us girls aren't as ignorant as we are supposed to be, that we've studied from the book of life while they were studying from books written by men. And said he, "No matter how wise man may be, life is the best teacher after all."

His words gave me lots of encouragement and I made my spiel, and if I have to say it myself I do think I made a good job of it. Of course, they can't really understand our position. How could they? They've never known what suffering and privation means, while us girls hadn't a bit of sweetness in all our lives.

I've spoken to those women for nigh a whole hour and when I got through the wise men were the loudest in their applause. I think it's because the people hear the truth so seldom now-a-days that when a body has the courage to speak right out they think it's great. But I couldn't help saying what I did, for it was just what I felt. Didn't even have a chance to see Jim today; will spend the day with him tomorrow.

January 16

Another Sunday passed. Tomorrow commences a new week and still no prospects, no hopes of settling this bitter fight. This is a hard, cold, merciless world, I must declare. But amid the narrow-minded, short-sighted mass stand out the few individuals—the forerunners of a better world to come. Oh, I'm so happy that I can honestly count my good Jim among them. There ain't a doubt in my mind but that Jim will always stand up for right against might. And the young girl whom I met at the entertainment this evening—I can imagine she'll get all that's coming to her, but she didn't seem to mind it one bit. Just got up from the chair and in her plain, simple way made a confession. Said that she was the daughter of the lawyer who served us with the injunction; told us that he was the noblest father living, but that was as far as his kindness went. She did not agree with him; she sympathized and felt for us girls, so not being able to do anything else she raffled off a little clock and made ten dollars, which she gave right there and then.

People like her have been hounded and abused and crucified before this, but they keep fighting for the truth until the majority have to think their way.

For ain't the freedom we are so loud in praising today something fought for by our forefathers a little over a century ago? The trouble with the truth is that it doesn't become popular until it has almost outlived its usefulness.

Here's my father—now that I've gone through all these hardships and am ready to start a new life, he's waking up; told Jim he'd like me to come home and if we're to be married it is not more than proper that I marry from my father's home. I'm afraid his proposal is a bit too late in the season. Where was he, my natural protector, when I was shoved in among all those rats—four and two-legged ones? Did he stretch out his hand to give me a bit of bread when I was almost perishing from hunger?

Lord! it's a good thing that nobody reads this notebook of mine—I scarcely think they could make anything out of it. Some might think me quite mad, and yet I'm keeping as closely to the subject as I possibly can, but I'm speaking of life as it strikes me every minute of the day and there're so many different things to think of that I'm at times quite puzzled to know what is of the most importance.

But then there's hardly anything I meet with now-a-days that ain't worth while recording—some day it may help to steady the ground under my children's feet. Us girls are the pioneer fighters for women's rights, for them rich women don't do much except talk a lot, while us girls show in reality how women can stand up for their rights.

I talked over the injunction business with Jim today. He

was just furious that these men should have the power to rob us of our freedom and forbid us to tell the truth. "Don't worry over it, Mary," Jim tried to console me, at the same time, "A new truth never had the majority with it; it's the dreamers, Mary, it's them that have dragged us up to our present position. I'm willing for them to call me a dreamer, to sneer and laugh at my ideals; he laughs best, Mary, who laughs last."

Lord! if men and women would only know how sweet it is to sit with the man you think most of in this great wide world and talk and reason and hope together. Yes, I'm positive that if people only knew what it means there wouldn't be half as many divorces as there are nowadays (and the poor don't get divorced, because they ain't got the cash for it).

I do wish I'd know how to rid ourselves of those blackguards, the leeches that stick like court plaster. One would think that they'd be tired, that now, since the majority of girls have won the strike they ought to go back where they came from, but that wouldn't be like them. I think what they want is to break the prestige of our having won. That's why they publish these reports that there ain't more than five hundred girls out on strike. What a lie! They know well that there are pretty near three thousand still outstanding. On the face of it, it would seem that they are our friends and want to boost us, but it ain't so. The people read that all the girls except a few hundred have gone back and stop sending in money, and this would mean, after all, that us girls will be starved into submission.

January 17

I don't know, I don't seem to understand it at all—there seems to be some undercurrent pulling things to pieces. If anything really useful for future guidance is started it's soon put a stop to. Here's that settled shops business. I wonder why it was dropped. Of course, it's a hard proposition and requires a great effort, but it'll pay in the end.

I don't understand why the smart people can't see it in this way. To my plain mind it seems absolutely necessary to meet with the settled shops. In fact, if I was in place of the League women I would devote most of the time to it. Met Kitty to-day—she had been out two weeks when her boss settled and she went back to work. I've become used to our girls and stood in the fight under fire all this while and talked to her as I would have talked to them; but, Lord! my words were Greek to her. Why, the girl was as ignorant as they make them. And she's only an example of the majority who went back before they had a chance to see and learn.

I told it to one of the women up town, but her answer was: "We ain't in no position to take it up just now." I wasn't as sure about it as she was. We must strike while the iron is red hot, while the other girls are still interested in the proposition, or we'll be obliged to close shop before very long. The woman argued, objected and tried to prove to me that I was wrong, but, with all due respect to her ability, I have not been able to convince myself that I wasn't right.

I left the League quite upset, and, as luck would have it, it never rains but it pours, into whom shall I run in but—my father. It may be wrong and yet I thought that meeting was the greatest piece of nuisance in the world. My father was ready to crush me down right there and then, when I refused point blank to go home. His words fell upon my head like a sledge hammer. First of all he wanted to know if I still persisted in having my own way. He taunted me with not having any feeling of gratitude or regard for the folk at home. Now, to be honest about it, I have loved my home as much as any girl does. It was nothing but my parents' treatment that turned me against it. People say there's a time when patience ceases to be a virtue, and this was exactly my case. My father thinks that I didn't act rightly towards him, but I must say the same of him. I told him the God's honest truth, but he called me a liar, scorned my ideals, mocked my hopes, threatened my freedom and drove me away from under his roof.

If a daughter wrongs her father she has the whole world against her; he has the right to deal with her according to his fancy. But if a father doubly wrongs his daughter his punishment is expected to be forgiveness on her part. I think it's because men are slaves to custom, after all. But I ain't. I shall never forgive him—never!

And I told Jim so, too, this evening on my way home. I was surprised to hear him plead with me that I make up with my father. In fact, it was almost a blow to me, for I've come to think of Jim as of a man always ready to stand up fearlessly on the side of the wronged party.

I told him that he had no right to reproach me with having hurt my father's feelings, for I was honest with my father. But, then, I knew Jim did it out of the goodness of his heart, and, I think, because he would like to see me out of this wretched place.

But I don't know as he has so much cause to complain. I let him treat me to supper every evening and pay my board to Mrs. Bloom, and actually took a dollar bill in cash from him.

I don't mean to say that I do him a favor, but it goes to show that I've come to think that he and I are one. That to stand high in his account I've set aside my principle not to take a farthing if I didn't work for it. I mean to do my share when Jim and I are married, and earn my living—every working-man's wife does, though not all may realize it.

But setting these little differences aside, I'm the happiest of all the brides I met yesterday at the City Hall. Our union will be tied by a double knot. Now since Jim, too, is converted to my way of thinking, we shall be one in spirit as well as body. But the fight is still on and tomorrow morning there is some more picketing to do.

January 18

This injunction business pops up like a rubber ball. Our women were all called to court this morning, kept for a couple of hours and sent home none the wiser for having been there. I think it's a scheme to keep them away from mischief. The bosses are foolish if they think it'll help them any. Pickets may go and pickets may come, but the fight will go on to a finish.

Had a talk with the German woman—she's the mother of a grown-up family. Her husband is a union man, and terribly opposed to women's activity outside of the home. But my German friend has a heart that goes out to us girls and she comes and helps us on the sly. She said that her children would be wild if they knew what she's doing around here. I like my friend, but somehow I have no sympathy for her in this case. If a mother can't bring up her own children in her way of thinking she has nobody to blame but herself.

Still and all, she is a heroine as well as the brave women who watch that place down on Walker street in spite of the orders of the court to refrain from appearing in that neighborhood.

As I was talking to Jim about it this morning I was trying hard to get up enough courage and ask him for some money— my shoes are on the blink. But do what I may, the words wouldn't escape from my throat, can't beg for myself. And yet our people say that I could take the first prize in begging for the cause. It's because I've learned to bury my personal feelings when the welfare of the other girls is at stake. I wouldn't mind to beg from night until morning and then from morning until night again, only to relieve the terrible hardships a bit. The poor devils have actually shrunk from the bitter cold and lack of food. The grocers and butchers in this neighborhood have their sympathy with us girls, but as one of them told me this morning, "I've been giving on credit until I'm broke. I know that these men and women mean well; that they are honest at heart, but where in the world will they get the money to pay back debts when they scarcely earn enough to go on from day to day?"

Three hundred girls went to work yesterday, and another two hundred today, but Mr. Hayman seems to be as firm as a rock. Many of the girls have left our ranks and I don't know how many more are preparing to leave. It's real hard. I first thought that the beginning is the hardest, but I know better now. It takes a great deal of nerve to keep up. And Jim—every time I meet him I read one and the same question in his pleading eyes: "Are you free to come yet?" It always makes me feel miserable. I know some people would call Jim Mr. Henpeck, but he ain't. He has more character than a dozen of those loud-mouthed yaps.

Jim himself said to me the other day: "Mary, I wouldn't think half as much of you if you weren't so firm to stick by the girls to the last. Only, Mary, a man is a man for all that. I'm longing for you every moment of my life."

I tell you what, it's a great thing to be in love, upon my word it is, especially if one loves a man like Jim. But, then, while love lasts every woman thinks that her man is just IT. Even that French dressmaker thought so, though her man was flirting with all the girls in the workroom right under her very nose.

But I ain't a bit jealous of Jim, and don't see much sense in being jealous, anyway. I think that when people get jealous of one another they may as well quit—what's the use, the confidence is gone?

Lord! I don't really know how daffy I am on Jim, until I catch myself thinking and writing of nothing but Jim. I mean to jot down about that lady lodge I visited this evening—it's worth while. "The Sisters of the Eagle," they style themselves. Parrots, is what I'd call them. It's to laugh to see those big, grown up women rigged out as if they were going to a masked ball. And how seriously they take it all. The fat mother superior in her square red cap and winged shaped sash across her shoulders acts as if she was the Czar of Russia. I think they've more secrets than brains in that lodge of theirs. A baker's dozen of women, each carting a big cake with her to the meeting, but none could spare a few cents for us girls.

January 19

Yes, I'm tired enough. One can't be of much good after putting in eight weeks like us girls did. And yet, while there's work to be done, I don't feel a bit weary; it's only when I get back here and stretch out on my narrow cot that it seems I could remain here forever.

For the first two weeks of my striking career I saw nothing before me but the miserable conditions of my companions and didn't even once think of my own health. How could I? Then came the quarrel with Jim and the family and I had still less time to bother about myself. The surroundings I've found myself in didn't tend to improve my health, nor did the week in prison. And today I almost feel guilty to burden Jim with a wreck of a woman.

I ain't the only one that broke down, either. They say Elizabeth is down and out and Leonora looks as though she's within an inch of the grave, and Helen—I really don't know how that girl lives; she don't eat anything the whole day long, for she's so upset that her stomach won't digest any food at all.

But I suppose we'll all keep up to the end. It can't last much longer after all—the season's now in full swing, the orders have to go out. What those bosses don't resort to! Helen drew my attention to an advertisement in one of the newspapers this morning. The Triangle wants waist makers, promising them from fifteen to twenty dollars weekly, free lunch and dancing during the noon hour.

No wonder they're so anxious to get workers. Their place has been closed the fourth month. I met several of their strikers today, and, upon my word, they didn't seem half as upset as their bosses. Only that their faces have dwindled down almost to nothing and their clothes are so shabby that they could hardly get work in a decent place. I guess that's just how tramps are made—a man loses his job and walks around looking for another until the clothing wears out and the man has to say farewell to his former surroundings, for everybody commences to look upon him with suspicion.

Met John. He has been down with fever for over four weeks. Got sick while doing work for the union at the rate of twenty-three hours a day. He got on the job the very first day and stayed there in that close office; didn't hardly eat anything, and worked and worried with the result that he had to be carried off in a stretcher.

The Lord bless him. He is one of the nameless ones who do their work not for reward or glory, but only for the good of mankind. When I looked at his thin face and staring eyes I was thankful that it fell to my lot to know the man. I'm sure the world will be the better for him having lived in it.

While I was talking to John who should come in but Sam that worked for Lefcovitch? Sam, he's still out and his wife is now working and supporting the two. Sam felt rather embarrassed when he told it to us, but I don't see why he should be. I know I'd rather go to work any time than see Jim scabbing.

It's enough to give one the blues to get into any of the halls nowadays. The few girls still out wander about like forlorn sheep. Some of them seem to be resigned to their fate, others are simply stupefied from suffering and just perform their duty automatically.

God! what a terrible, bloodless tragedy this strike of ours turned out to be! Yes, I'm right in saying bloodless, for there ain't a bit of blood left in the girls. I don't know, but I had a funny day and can't help seeing everything from the dark side. I guess it's because Jim didn't come 'round.

Strange as it may seem, in spite of my moods and thoughts, I ain't a bit sorry for having struck. For the last few years things have been getting steadily worse. Wages decreasing and the cost of living getting higher. Many of the people that I've met since the strike have lost half of their families through nothing but starvation. Why, even the charities reported that this year is the worst ever. It was about time that somebody should protest and I'm glad that us girls were brave enough to do it, even if many will have to pay with their life for it. I'm willing to forfeit mine.

January 20

At Elizabeth's suggestion I went into a paper box factory to ask for a job. Even from the outside the place is enough to give you the shivers. It looks as old and dilapidated that a-body can't help fearing that it may topple over any time.

But then the outside ain't in it when you see the inside—the smell of paste is enough to kill a hog, the filth around the table is knee deep and the type of girls that works there reminds you of a lot of haunted animals that have been driven to their last resource. And no wonder! I don't really see how anybody with a bit of hope for the future can consent to remain in this living hell. That's just what it is; even the workhouse is much preferable to this place—it's dirtier than the former. You can't say a word the whole day long and the wages paid for the work don't afford better food than they give at the workhouse.

I didn't remain there more than a half an hour. The boss offered me a dollar and a half per week. God! I first wept and then cursed when I left the miserable place. There seems to be no end to the depth of suffering. Is it possible that the nation as a whole is ignorant of it all? How dare they to cry out against white slavery when girls are driven to it with the strong whip of hunger? Lord! I'm ready to embrace anything which promises a remedy for the aching hearts, relief from the wholesale starvation.

It seems to me that the working people won't be ground to

dust much longer. They bore about as much as their nature can stand; their ever rising fury is bound to break out any day.

Jim was wild at my going when he saw the effect it had upon me. "God bless you, child," said he. "I know it's all true. I'm myself of the opinion that we're on the eve of great changes, but then—you must save yourself for bigger things."

"But, Jim, Jim," I pleaded. "What are we coming to? Jim, my boy, where is the remedy?" And even as I asked him that question I seemed to hear the echo of a great uprising coming from afar and I can hear it even now—it keeps ringing in my ears all the time.

Well, whatever may happen, I'm happy in the thought that I won't have to fight alone much longer. It will always be Jim and I—I and Jim. It is a sin for me to go on in that manner. I know that I must not cry. I must not give way. There's lots of work ahead for both of us. But, then, the surroundings make me so wretched, so wretched! I talk to the girls about sticking it out, and at the same time can't help thinking that I'm wrong. They have but one life to live, why increase their misery? They won't see better times, at any rate.

I'm preaching the truth just the same. And truth is best all the time. But, then, I'm so mixed up that I don't rightly know what I mean. And what is the wonder! There's poor Ray coughing away her last days, and Minnie and Mrs. Bloom with her many sorrows and the money, too, stopped coming in. Saw Mr. Shindler this afternoon. The man is almost mad from despair, but I think it's their own fault in a way. Why keep an army of walking delegates and pay each from fifteen to eighteen dollars per week? I wouldn't give them five cents, if I had my say. They don't know the first thing how to treat us girls. I'm pretty sure that the League women would have done the work voluntarily, without a cent's pay.

Jim didn't like my saying this, but I'm a partner to this striking game and have a right to judge what I think is wrong.

I hope Jim's right and I may be wrong, but them paid officials ain't no better than a sponge for sucking up money. I wouldn't care a snap if it wasn't needed to keep up life. I know some girls that have received only three dollars benefit for the whole time of the strike. God! three dollars for eight weeks! What didn't these poor kids have to endure? Even I myself couldn't commence to understand it, for I stayed home for a while, then had enough to take to the uncle for a couple of weeks, and now Jim's helping me out and still and all, I went hungry and cold many a day. But they—they hadn't a drop of help from anywhere.

I don't know what is coming over me. I can't do no good by saying all these things. Perhaps it's the last bit of suffering. Maybe things will take a better turn before long.

January 21

Lord! I haven't felt as good in many a day. Mr. Hayman sent word this afternoon that he would like to see a committee. I do hope they may come to some settlement. I'm almost sure that if he was to give in the others wouldn't keep back much longer. As it is, people say that there ain't more than eighteen bosses left in the whole organization.

I don't wonder one bit that they couldn't exist. How could they, when they're all engaged in a hair-pulling match, each trying to outdo the other? It's entirely different with us girls. We have nothing to fight each other for. From the very first day we came out on strike all of us, well paid and poorly paid, girls were determined to stand or fall together.

Some blame us girls for having started this whole affair. They claim that it's going to hurt everybody and won't help us. Well, I beg to differ. It helped us already—twenty-one thousand people enrolled on the union books, about seventeen thousand back to work under agreements with the bosses, the remainder still fighting and at the same time being molded into types that will withstand any fire.

When us girls saw the bright light for the first time we had to rub our eyes; we could hardly see at all—everything seemed so strange. We strained our ears, but were deaf to the things preached to us. Gradually as the days went by we commenced to learn, and now—well, well, I have to laugh. I'm considered too radical by some of our League women.

It's strange about those very women—they go around the poor and wretched, see and know all the misery and injustice, deplore it, but when it comes to take a stand, to speak the truth, they shrink back from doing it. Of course, they ain't the majority, but they're the ones that's got the money, and that counts nowadays.

Why, even at this late date, after all the clubbings and arrests and other abuses, after the steady persecution and injunctions, some of our would-be well-wishers try to excuse the people and judges, mingle with them in society and look upon us that speak up without fear as if we were in the way.

I can just imagine what Mr. Hayman felt when he had to send for us after all. Why, the man is as stubborn as a mule. I suppose he was pressed real hard. And just because our girls stuck together. I don't see why in the world the entire striking crowd didn't understand it that way. Here is Susie from the Daisy Waist Company—poor kid! it's terrible to see her wander around from place to place; only three of them still outstanding—the others went back scabbing. Of course, I can't blame the girl for refusing to follow them. I don't see how as I would do it, either. But, then, if we use some common sense it's easy to realize that Susie can't hope for a settlement; that she don't really help us one bit by standing out.

I just told her to come and stay with us, the stray duckling that she is. If Mr. Hayman will settle we'll manage to smuggle her in. It's a mighty good thing to have one like her in the workroom—she surely knows what she wants.

Lord! but Jim was happy when I told him the glad news. I thought he'd smother me with kisses. I'm a funny goose, I am. I feel embarrassed to say a word about our love making, even here on paper. And yet, it is only natural. I'm sure there ain't nothing to be ashamed of. Mrs. Bloom wanted to know the other day whether I've grown so cold that nothing in this wide world can heat me up any longer. She never saw me behave different to Jim than I do to the rest of them. The idea! I think it's terrible, this public love making, as if a-body needs carry one's feelings on the sleeve.

Jim fully agrees with me. Not by word or motion does he betray his passion before others. He makes up for it, though, when we are alone. I think the man would go mad or commit suicide if he was to lose me now. I'm beginning to wonder whether he is so radical because he loves me, or he loves me so because I'm as radical as he is. I say and repeat the word radical and, upon my word, I do not know what it really means, only people have been calling us that. I'm pretty rusty in book knowledge, but I mean to make it up when Jim and I build our little nest.

January 22

I thought so. Bill said that Hayman behaved like a madman. He swore and stamped his feet and cursed—just because he has to bend a little. His feelings are hurt, he said. And what about ours? Let him look back and think of the many hours, and days, and weeks, and years that us girls had to bow before his temper. So far nothing came out of that conference—Bill ain't the kind to monkey and dilly dally with the bosses. You have either to sign the union agreement or we'll keep fighting you. That's just what he said. And Hayman told him to go to ———— .

I think it's better not to have any hopes than to have them and lose them as we did our hope of settlement today. I couldn't make myself say a word to the girls, for fear we'd all burst out crying. Many a one sat there biting her lips as hard as she could.

I ran out of the meeting room and outside the door came face to face with Corrola—she's a brick, I must say. Here's a girl who's got more money than she will ever be able to spend, no matter what she does with it. To think of it, that she should go in and spend three months in a New York laundry, but that's just what Corrola did, and during the hot summer months at that. She wanted to find out for herself the real life of the working girl.

And now, since the beginning of the strike, Corrola has been spending her days and nights in the courts—bailing us out as fast as she could sign the papers. I put my head on Corrola's shoulder and had a good cry. I was crying not only for myself, but for Ray and Mrs. Bloom, Minnie and Dutch Annie, poor old Martha and all the rest who have to suffer in order that others may enjoy.

Hadn't the heart to tell the folks here that the conference fell flat. Mrs. Bloom got some supper on account of our possible settlement—promised the grocer to pay him next week when Ray and I will get our wages. I wonder how many more weeks will pass before we get any wages? It's surprising how much love this woman bears in her wounded heart. I know and had quite a share of it since I am here.

This evening Jim and I went to Cooper Union to hear the Socialist boss of Milwaukee. I tell you what—he looks and acts the boss every inch of it, but if that man ain't got brains and ability to do things I don't know who has.

I ain't a bit surprised that there are so many Socialists in his city—I think he can convince any one that the only hope for the working people lies in a clean sweep. Upon my word, after the many weeks of strike this has almost settled Jim and me—we're about ready to join the great army of comrades.

It may be silly, but I have a soft spot for that word—kept

calling Jim that way while he was taking me home. But Jim, he said I can't scare him by it—that the world as it goes today is either right or wrong, and it certainly can't be right, or my experience couldn't have taken place; then, if it is wrong— what is an honest man and woman to do but join hands with all those who want to right the wrong.

I didn't say much to my good, noble Jim, only nodded my head in approval, for I knew he was right. How can a body look on at our girls who are doomed to suffering from their very cradle and remain indifferent, unless as one of the so-called labor leaders told me not long ago: "I've killed my sentiment many years before this." But what care I for labor leaders or no labor leader as long as Jim and I understand each other fully.

I must have been born in a shirt, am what people would call a fortune child as compared with the other girls. Here's Lilly, for instance—she is all alone in this world, not a kin or friend to cling to. I can't really understand how she managed to push through all this while. With her it's gloom all the time; not a ray of sunshine from anywheres—she's the real hall bedroom girl. God! it's only by a hair's breadth that I've escaped being dragged into this horror. Where would I be today if not for Jim. My own dear Jim, no wonder I've hugged him so close to me before I let him go this evening. Honestly, it's almost a sin to have such fits of happiness amidst all this worry and trouble.

January 23

All comes to him who works for it! All hail to us girls—we got what we wanted—Mr. Hayman had to sign the agreement after all. Oh, I begged and coaxed them and they took me along on the committee—just wanted to see for myself how he behaved. Well, well, he made me think of the animals at the circus—jumped and kicked and gnawed his teeth to the very last moment—but us girls had the strong whip over him—he must send out his orders and pride must go. Ours went long ago—we needed bread to keep up our life. And why should we alone suffer all the time?

I know that it has been going on that way for a long, long while—the poor worked and suffered and watched their children growing pale from lack of food and ill health. But still they went on uncomplaining—it's all because there's a dark curtain hung over their tired eyes and they don't see natural things in their natural light. And yet—the contrast is getting too great. I know it's nothing but the terrible contrast that helped open my eyes and Jim's.

Lord! I never thought of it to this very minute. Why, upon my word, this is supposed to be my wedding day! But how could I think of myself at such a critical moment—what is one little tree in this great forest of people? It's the girls! Oh, the girls, they were so happy that they cried for joy. And they've all grown so dear to me. It may be foolish, but I really dislike the idea of parting with them—they have been the means of awakening me to a fuller, better life. They are to go on working and slaving day in and day out, too busy to think of leisure by day and too tired to get much rest by night.

One would scarcely think that two months could work such wonders in a person, but it's exactly two months today since I left Hayman's; I couldn't hardly believe it myself, only for my scribbling which I have been doing day by day. Jim and I read it over the other night. Yes, Jim—he doesn't know yet what happened—I ran straight home as soon as I informed the girls. Ray is sick in bed—I thought that the glad news may act like medicine.

I don't know, I just hate to think of it—but the relief may have come too late. God! my heart almost breaks for her; nobody knows how I've come to love that sweet girl. And her kind mother—herself worn out by hunger and bending under unbearable burden she watches at the sick bed of her first born, her hope, her pride. The doctor said Ray needs good nourishment—what mocking advice in this household!

I know, I've promised Jim to marry him on the day Mr. Hayman settles with us girls. I shall keep my promise; in fact, I'm happy to do it—I'm perhaps as anxious for the event as he himself. But there's one thing Jim can't refuse me on my wedding day—he, too, will have to make a promise. I shall not leave Ray at her death bed, and Mrs. Bloom and the little ones, they were my only consolation in the hour of sorrow. I'm bound to do something for them, their suffering has reached the summit.

Jim'll come and stay with me here, and we'll pay Mrs. Bloom board and our share of the rent, and I'll go down to Hayman's and keep Ray's place for her until she's well enough to do it herself. I know Jim won't like it, but his noble heart and good common sense will do the job for me.

I'm a bit nervous—Jim's liable to drop in any moment—we have the license ready, and no matter how late it might be, he will insist upon the fulfillment of my promise this very evening.

Strange—I love, I adore Jim. I'd die if I was to be prevented from marrying him, and yet—now on the threshold of the event itself I'm torn asunder by a thousand thoughts and fears and hopes—I'm entering upon an entirely new path of life. I'm assuming responsibilities I know nothing of. Will I be equal to my task?

I'm inclined to think I shall. I've thought it all over many, many times; I think every girl should, and I mean to bring myself to the point where I could be a real friend and companion to Jim. I shall be with him in the hour of joy and in the hour of sorrow. I shall soothe and comfort him, consult and advise. For one thing—I know Jim will meet me exactly on the same grounds—we will be, we must be, happy.

This edition of *The Diary of a Shirtwaist Striker* is designed by Kat Dalton. The text has been reset, but except for typographical errors, it is exactly as it appeared in the original edition, published by the Cooperative Press in 1910. The cover photo is used with permission of Brown Brothers.

Library of Congress Cataloging-in-Publication Data
Malkiel, Theresa Serber.
    The diary of a shirtwaist striker / Theresa Serber Malkiel : introductory essay by Françoise Basch.
        p.   cm. — (Literature of American labor series)
    Includes bibliographical references.
    ISBN 0–87546–168–9 (pbk. : acid free)
    1. Strikes and lockouts—Clothing trade—New York (N.Y.)--History—20th century—Fiction.   I. Basch, Françoise. II. Title.
III. Series: Literature of American labor.
PS3525.A446D53   1990
813'.52—dc20   90–41090